Freshwater Fishing
Secrets II

Freshwater Fishing Secrets II

Complete Angler's Library®
North American Fishing Club
Minneapolis, Minnesota

Freshwater Fishing Secrets II

Copyright © 1992, North American Fishing Club

Library of Congress Catalog Card Number 92-61041
ISBN 0-914697-48-X

Printed in U.S.A.
6   7   8   9

Contents

Acknowledgments

The North American Fishing Club would like to thank all those who have helped make this book a reality.

Wildlife artist Virgil Beck created the cover art. Artist David Rottinghaus provided all illustrations. Photos, in addition to the authors', were provided by Beth Bucher, *North American Fisherman* Editor Steve Pennaz, Zebco Corporation and Henry F. Zeman.

And, a special thanks goes to the NAFC's publication staff for all their efforts: Publisher Mark LaBarbera, *North American Fisherman* Editor Steve Pennaz, Managing Editor of Books Ron Larsen, Associate Editor of Books Colleen Ferguson and Art Director Dean Peters. Thanks also to Vice President of Product Marketing Mike Vail, Marketing Manager Cal Franklin and Marketing Project Coordinator Laura Resnik.

Foreword

Earlier in history of the Complete Angler's Library we produced a book titled *Freshwater Fishing Secrets* which highlighted the techniques and tactics of top fishermen across the country. It, like our official club publication, *North American Fisherman*, covers a wide variety of fish species, including bass, walleye, catfish, panfish and more. NAFC Members loved it. Letters poured in from across the country asking if we could do another book following the same format.

You are holding that book.

Like the original *Freshwater Fishing Secrets* book, *Freshwater Fishing Secrets II* will share the hottest methods of the hottest fishermen around. And like the original book, most of the men featured are not nationally known. These are the guys who dominate their local angling scenes. A few of them are professional guides or charter service operators, but most of them are not. Some of them fish tournaments, though not on a professional basis.

So who are these guys? Great anglers who have effective fishing techniques to share but who have never before been given the opportunity. And unlike professionals who have sponsors to keep happy, these anglers don't have to hold back information. They can tell it like it is because they have nothing to lose.

In this book you'll meet:

● Giant-bass expert Bob Crupi, an NAFC Member and policeman from California who has nearly shattered the world record on at least three occasions in recent years—an incredible feat. His largest fish to date weighed 22.01 pounds, missing the record by a mere four ounces. He released the fish!

You'll learn all about Bob's secrets for catching fish like these in Chapter 1.

● Crappie expert Charlie Ingram who knocks the socks off mid-summer reservoir crappies with jigging spoons. Yes, I said jigging spoons. This just may be the ticket to taking those fish many anglers have trouble catching during the hot summer months.

● Pennsylvania's flathead-catfish enthusiast Jim Rogers who finds no greater thrill than catching monster cats from heavily fished waters. If you like fishing huge cats you won't want to miss this one.

● River-walleye expert Dave Lincoln, who, with friend and tournament partner Art Lehrman, has dominated river-walleye tournaments across the Midwest in recent years. He'll share secrets that I guarantee will make you a better river-walleye angler—no matter where you live!

● Charter captain Bob Cinelli, a lake trout and salmon guide on mighty Lake Ontario. I have fished with Bob and can personally attest to his uncanny ability to find and catch fish. He'll share his methods on how to combat the negative effects of current, and help you develop a spoon program that will increase your Great Lakes success.

● Joe Bucher, a frequent contributor to *North American Fisherman* and co-author of the Complete Angler's Library title *Hunting Trophy Muskies & Northerns*. Joe is one of the finest muskie anglers in the world. He has had numerous five- and six-fish days despite fishing some of the hardest-pounded waters in the country. Joe has unlocked the secrets of open-water monster muskies and the tips he shares may just lead you to the fish of a lifetime.

● Arthur Kelso, a striper expert who has tremendous success finding and catching old linesides in boiling tailrace areas. This isn't easy fishing, but the rewards are huge for those willing to make the investment.

And a whole lot more!

And like the original book, *Freshwater Fishing Secrets II* will put you on the water with these men. You'll learn how they catch more and bigger fish than everyone else. You'll also discover what makes these anglers tick through the intimate glimpses supplied by our authors. All are seasoned and respected writers who are familiar with the water and recognize the qualities that make these anglers experts in their field.

I hope you enjoy *Freshwater Fishing Secrets II* as much as we've enjoyed working on it!

Steve Pennaz
Executive Director
North American Fishing Club

Largemouth
And Smallmouth Bass

1

Chasing World-Record Bass

by Bob Sarber

Being a well-decorated captor of giant largemouth bass, Bob Crupi should be satisfied with his accomplishments. But Crupi's success has only fueled his desire to ascend to the next level. "That big fish is still out there, so there is still a goal," he insists. "And I still have the desire."

Crupi wants the new world record—a largemouth bass heavier than the 22-pound, 4-ounce beauty caught by George W. Perry in 1932. On two occasions, Crupi has been close to breaking Perry's record.

The first near-miss was on March 9, 1990. His five-fish limit totaled 72 pounds, including a bodacious fish tipping the scales at more than 21 pounds.

Then, on March 12, 1991, Crupi reeled in a bigger prize. Fishing alone off a point, he hooked, fought and landed a 22-pound largemouth. After carefully weighing, measuring and photographing the fish, he promptly released it in the approximate area of its capture.

His releasing a fish within four ounces of the world record was at first viewed curiously, even suspiciously. Many wondered how he could do such a thing. "Hey," Crupi responded, "I did what we're going to have to do if we are to have world-class fish in the future."

Crupi will be looking for that giant fish he returned to the water, hoping that it has gained a pound or two since its release. Should he catch it, and find that it has indeed added to its former

This is just one of the more than 50 largemouths over 10 pounds that Bob Crupi has taken during his quest for the world's largest fish. He has missed obtaining the world record by a mere four ounces.

Lake Castaic's rugged look belies the fact that it is only an hour's drive north of the nation's second-largest city, Los Angeles. The lake is home to some huge largemouth bass.

27½-inch girth, you'll be hearing a lot about Bob Crupi, recreational fisherman and 18-year veteran of the Los Angeles Police Department.

Crupi has caught 52 largemouths that have topped the 10-pound mark—six of them have weighed more than 15 pounds. He holds International Game Fish Association (IGFA) line-class world records for largemouth bass in the 4-pound-, 12-pound- and 16-pound-test categories. His mastery of catching trophy largemouths evolves from boyhood fishing trips in his native Long Island, New York.

When he was 16, Crupi and his family moved to southern California, where Crupi was within driving distance of some of the biggest bass in the world.

He first fished lakes around San Diego (they surrendered some big fish), then concentrated on Lake Casitas in Ventura County. In 1976, Crupi discovered Lake Castaic in Los Angeles County; the discovery changed both the lake and the angler.

Crupi and Castaic merged at a time when both were on the brink of maturity—Crupi as an angler and Castaic as a trophy bass fishery. Crupi spent a lot of time learning about the lake and experimenting with the new knowledge. In 1981, he caught what was then a lake record 14-pound, 14-ounce largemouth. Since then, he has caught six heavier fish.

Castaic is a canyon-like, 2,000-acre reservoir approximately 40 miles north of Los Angeles. Obviously, it is fertile water, but not just anybody is going to take 20-plus-pound bass out of it. Located near the nation's second largest city, Castaic is often congested. Void of shoreline structure, the lake is an underwater world consisting primarily of points, auxiliary points, ledges and drop-offs.

"The guy who fishes only now and then is not going to be as consistently successful as the guy who can get out there several times a week," insists Crupi, whose work schedule allows ample daylight hours to spend on the water.

Residing within a mile of the lake, Crupi can monitor the environmental variables that can change daily. Certain areas produce fish when the wind blows a specific direction; other spots are more sensitive to current direction. And because Castaic is a domestic water-supply facility on the state aqueduct system, its water level fluctuates drastically. "You've got to pay attention to nature," Crupi says.

When Crupi launches out, he first reads the prevailing weather conditions. Then, knowing all the spots that produce big fish, Crupi quickly eliminates several from consideration based on the current conditions.

For example, he checks his paper-graph sonar to determine the depth at which fish are stratified. Because he knows about productive structure at specific depths (according to the water level on a given day), he can head quickly to the most promising spots. Each spot Crupi fishes has its own personality and must be studied in detail. Sometimes the most subtle characteristics of structure signal profitable fishing.

Crupi concedes that his bass fishing has consisted of "a lot of trial and error." However, he also admits to accepting helpful hints from some very sharp fishermen. Crupi credits Danny Kadota with teaching him the most. Kadota, the same age as Crupi, is a former saltwater charter-boat skipper who would fish Castaic on the days he wasn't at sea. Crupi became a twice-a-month charter passenger of Kadota's, and they would frequently huddle in the wheelhouse during these saltwater excursions, discussing their respective approaches to fishing.

An outstanding saltwater fisherman, Kadota successfully incorporated many of his sea strategies into his big-bass game plan. "Fish are fish," he theorizes. "Whether they are largemouth bass or bluefin tuna, they're a lot the same."

Apparently, Kadota's thinking is sound. He has taken about 90 largemouths over 10 pounds, including a 19.04-pounder that was the IGFA 20-pound line-class world record.

Crupi's approach to Castaic's bass begins with using live bait—mostly waterdogs or mudsuckers. But when the fish are in their prespawn period (mid-December through mid-March), they display a distinct preference for crayfish. Crupi happily accommodates them, converting his garage into a refuge for the crustaceans (which he refers to as "ammo").

Bob Crupi and his bass-fishing mentor, Danny Kadota (left), pose with bass that would be career achievements for most anglers. Kadota applies tactics that he developed in saltwater.

Crupi shows the correct way to hook a crayfish. If the bait is hooked through its crown, rather than through its tail, it will move naturally, and its movements will attract largemouths.

Crupi admits he hasn't always been successful with crayfish. "I used to hook them through the tail," he says, "and when a bass would hit, I would let it run with the bait before I set the hook. Man, that was stupid!"

Now a wiser crayfish fisherman, Crupi hooks the bait through the crown that extends down between its eyes. That arrangement, he thinks, lets the bait move more freely and gives it a more natural look. He also sets the hook immediately upon detecting a bite.

Rigging is simple. The main line, typically 8-, 10-, or 12-pound test, ties directly to a No. 2 or No. 4 hook. Unless bass are real shallow and looking to eat the first thing that hits the water, Crupi attaches a small split shot 18 inches above the hook.

Rigging is the only thing simple about the bait's use, however.

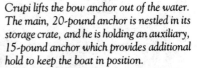

Crupi lifts the bow anchor out of the water. The main, 20-pound anchor is nestled in its storage crate, and he is holding an auxiliary, 15-pound anchor which provides additional hold to keep the boat in position.

Crupi works diligently through precise boat positioning to put the bait exactly where he wants it. This is where he leans heavily on Kadota's lessons. According to Kadota, "We had a philosophy on the ocean that holds true on freshwater—the farther away you can be from a spot and still get a bait on it, the better those fish are going to bite."

Crupi's two 20-pounders bit when he was positioned outside (in deeper water) and was casting toward the shallows. It gets far more complicated than that, though, because Crupi doesn't randomly cast to shallow water but to very specific locations. If there's a point sinking down into the water, Crupi must determine which side of the point to position on and which side of the point to cast to.

Crupi positions upcurrent from the spot he fishes, then he lets the current carry his bait to the promising structure. He learned from Kadota that baitfish travel with the current, and predator fish face into it.

To position a boat so precisely takes mental and physical stamina, but making the extra effort is worthwhile, according to Crupi, because the crayfish is a crawling bait, not a swimming bait. Being dragged by the boat's swing gives the crayfish an unnatural appearance. For this reason, the boat must be kept mo-

Proper Boat Positioning For Trophy Bass

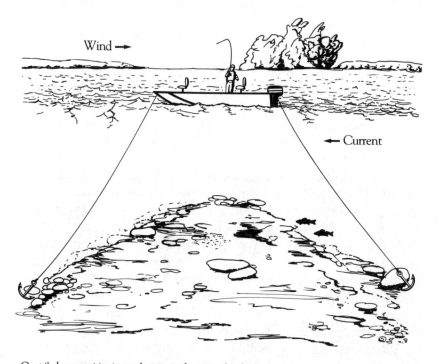

Crupi's boat-positioning technique is shown in this diagram. A key to its success is keeping the anchors and their lines as far from the spot being fished as is physically possible.

tionless. Crupi's nifty double-anchoring technique ensures that it will be.

After finding the spot he wants to fish and determining current direction, Crupi drops a marker buoy for his boat. If possible, he points the bow into the wind. Then Crupi circles the buoy, drops a stern anchor 100 feet upcurrent from the buoy, and moves slowly forward, dropping the bow anchor 100 feet downcurrent from the buoy. Pulling back on the stern anchorline until the boat sits alongside the buoy, he then pulls up snug on the bow anchor line and ties off.

Considerable strategy goes into placing the two U.S. Navy-style anchors. Certainly, Crupi wants to keep the anchors as far from the spot as he can so they won't block any access routes or spook fish in the area. And he wants to make sure the anchor lines won't interfere when he is fighting a fish.

With this setup, Crupi can make minor adjustments, accommodating environmental changes. If current switches so that he needs to reposition and fish a different part of that structure, he can loosen line on one anchor and pull up on the other in a kind of pulley-like manner.

Having his boat precisely positioned and knowing where he wants his bait, Crupi is ready to cast. Now the pursuit of big bass becomes a matter of touch. From the moment the bait hits the water, Crupi must determine through feel what it may be telling him. "That's the biggest advantage in fishing live bait," he says, " ... being able to feel its emotion."

A crayfish's emotions are expressed through the "thumps" of its tail. The thumps are transmitted in various frequencies, and each frequency carries a meaning. One frequency might represent a crayfish trying to crawl into a bed of rocks. In this case, Crupi with a gentle lifting of the rodtip will influence it away from such an area. Another frequency can be interpreted as restlessness. Crupi responds by letting the bait roam where it wants. Finally, a "fear" frequency is one that excites Crupi. There is no feeling quite like a crayfish that knows it is about to be eaten. And when that sensation occurs, Crupi gets ready to sink the hook.

Of course, it also is possible that the bait is exhibiting no emotion. Then Crupi assumes the bait is either unattractive or in water devoid of hungry predators. He first tries changing bait and if there is still no action, he changes location.

For the most part, Crupi works a bait back toward him with slow, short lifts. The moment a bait emits any kind of excitement, though, he pauses so the bait can behave naturally.

Crupi has hooked his two biggest fish at different depths. The 21-pounder was hooked in 5 feet of water, and the 22-pounder at about 35 feet. Their fights lacked the excitement found in facing 8- to 12-pound fish. When these big, portly fish are hooked, they rely on their massive bulk to power them into deeper water, and the battle is largely an up-and-down affair.

Crupi works to turn the fish's head toward him, so that each flip of the fish's tail brings it closer to him. With the fish facing him, Crupi begins to short-pump the rod—lifting, then reeling down in short, steady, brisk increments.

The blend of sensitivity and power required for hooking, and then battling giant bass requires careful tackle selection. Rods must be light enough to transmit the crayfish's emotions, yet have the strength to withstand the big fish's struggle for freedom. After sampling many different rods, Crupi has settled on the G. Loomis IMX series of casting rods and matches particular models to the line size he is using. "I can't believe how much my percentage of hooked fish has gone up since I started using the rods," says Crupi. "And it's only because I have so much more feel."

Reels must perform dependably. They must cast lightweight crayfish with some degree of distance, and their gearing and drag systems must offer strong and smooth support. The Daiwa PMF-1000, a reel no longer produced, retired as Crupi's champion in this regard. He now uses the new, lightweight baitcasting reels developed by Shimano.

Finally, Crupi stresses the importance of using monofilament that won't stretch when the hook is set. Clear Berkley XT is used a lot at Castaic for this reason. Crupi has recently changed to TripleFish Camoescent line, a color-coded, camouflaged line.

Along with experience and confidence in his tackle, a big-bass angler relies heavily on luck, according to Crupi. "There's no room for any error, even the slightest," Crupi says. "I feel real fortunate to have caught my last fish (the 22-pounder). I was fishing too heavy structure with too light of line. There was a tree there, and twice I felt the fish bulldog down to it—I actually felt the line rub against it. But, hey, I was lucky."

2

Solving The Clearwater Mystery

by Tony Mandile

Fish the wood. Throw into the duckweed. Look for the places where the creeks come in. Stick to the hydrilla. Worm the stained water. Not too surprisingly, most fishermen in the eastern half of the country are quite familiar with these suggestions. They are some of the tried-and-true ways for catching largemouth bass in the Midwest, South and East. But when the same fishermen move west, they find big reservoirs—huge, bathtub-like impoundments with little cover. Worst of all, the lakes are deep and crystal clear.

These conditions can intimidate even the well-traveled tournament angler who is not accustomed to being able to see his quarry swimming 15 feet beneath the surface. Sometimes he is intimidated enough to mutter, "Nah, I knew how to fish the lake; the fish were just too finicky." Yet most anglers who finish high in the standings, however, obviously find a way to catch uncooperative fish. Most likely, they recall previous experiences under similar conditions, allowing them to repeat it. I attended the Redman All-American tournament at Lake Havasu (on the Arizona-California border) as a press observer a few years ago and spent two days with competitors from Missouri and Georgia. Neither of them had ever fished gin-clear lakes comparable to Havasu. So away from their home ranges, they were somewhat lost. They spent a major part of their day searching for places resembling those they fished "back East." Both finished far down in the list of the 50 or so competing anglers.

Jerry Suk is one professional fisherman who has solved the mystery of taking bass in clear waters. He consistently places in tournaments held on Western clearwater lakes.

Solving The Clearwater Mystery

The fish were there, though. Otherwise, many of the daily limits taken by the top finishers, like Rick Clunn who took home the first-place money, would have been nonexistent. Clunn had lots of experience fishing in the West, and he knew where and how to catch fish in Havasu's clear water.

And so does Jerry Suk, who is a regular competitor on Arizona's Allstar Bass tournament circuit and its 1991 Angler of the Year. Suk consistently makes the top five and twice has finished second in all-star tournaments at Havasu.

"Bass in clear water are both uniquely vulnerable under certain conditions and quite wary under others," Suk says. "When we can't catch them, we too often look for excuses to save a fractured ego. But normally they are right where they belong and doing the same things they would do in stained or muddy water—feeding and hiding. The answer is simple. Just figure out where those places are and fish them."

Suk's solution is quite simple and goes right to the point: Find the cover most fish are using.

"When you fish clear lakes like Havasu, Powell or Mead over the years," he says, "you gradually learn how bass react. You see how they use depth, structure and whatever type of cover or vegetation that is available. Of course, the foods bass favor generally stay in the same places."

Clear water means, for most fishermen, being able to see a light-colored object at a depth of 5 feet or more. The extent of clarity will affect the fish's choice of hiding places and its ability to detect anything suspicious, including the line leading to a lure. Suk feels the line can have a definite effect.

"In today's highly competitive fishing environment, where an increasing number of tournament and weekend anglers vie for fishing spots and a finite number of fish," he says, "it's important to have an edge. There's no use throwing the right lure to the right spot if your line is scaring fish.

"When bass are close enough to see your lure, they are close enough to see your line, too," Suk explained. "In most waters, the range a bass can see varies from 6 inches to 2 feet, which means it can see varying lengths of line, as well. Most likely when it gets close to the lure in murky water, it might only see the knot and a couple of inches of line. It's hardly anything to get worked up about, though, because by then the fish has basically committed

Complete Angler's Library

Taking bass in clear waters such as this is a matter of paying attention to details. Anglers need to be concerned about the fish seeing the line; hence, line size and color are important.

to the lure. In clear water, though, it might see the line from the knot to your reel from a long way off."

This relationship between water clarity and the amount of line that bass possibly see has caused many anglers to rely on a simple formula for selecting line; they use bright lines in stained or muddy water, smoky colors in clear water and clear line as an all-around choice.

Suk, however, feels color isn't as important as line size. He relies on Berkley's UltraThin, which is super clear for his light-line fishing, even though he doesn't think the line's color is as important as its thickness. "When it comes to line color," he says, "I generally go with 'it's better to be safe than sorry' but I pay a lot of attention to weight. If I'm fishing shoreline structure like rock rubble, I'll go to 8-pound test for working bottom-type lures. I al-

Suk often turns to a flipping technique for working whatever cover is available. The lure usually is only inches from the fish as it drops into the cover.

most always use a split shot or a Carolina rig for fishing these areas. I switch to 6-pound line and a spinning rig for light, in-line spinners, and move up to 20-pound test for flippin'.

Even in clear water, however, Suk turns to a highly visible line for flippin' because it "is a close-up technique where color makes little difference," he says. "The fish are normally only a few inches from the lure as it drops into the cover, and the area is usually very shaded. The fish either take it or they don't. Also, a slight line movement is frequently the only indication that a bass has taken your lure. By using bright-colored line, like Berkley's Trilene Hi-Vis, I can easily pick up the movement, even below the surface.

"One thing I do when I first start is make sure all the coils are out of the line. Even when you put new line on the night before, it will still have coils because of the weight. So I usually always pull it off a few feet at a time and then stretch it a bit. Of course, my first fish will do the same thing, but having the coils in the line until I hook one could delay the first fish."

Suk chooses his fishing spots and methods according to the lake and the weather. If he's at Havasu, he quickly races up the river end to the huge tule jungle. Once there, he turns to his favorite and most productive technique—flippin'.

"Bass in clearwater lakes will utilize cover just like they do elsewhere," he says, "and the tules provide some of the best they can find at Havasu. This is especially so on bright, sunny days. They will either go deep or move right into the middle of the tules. Even though the water is clear and shallow, the tules provide ample concealment and shade to make the bass feel at ease. And if you want to get them out of the latter, you have to get your bait into them. For me, flippin' is the most effective way to do it.

"Heck, even on the lakes with clear water, a lot of the bigger fish stay in shallow water among the rocks all year long. So flippin' among the rocks can also be productive, especially when the water level drops and leaves all the brush high and dry," he says.

Although flippin' began in other parts of the country, California's Dee Thomas popularized the technique using the original Fenwick Flippin' Stik. Others, including Dave Gliebe, Gary Klein and Rich Tauber, followed his lead and successfully flipped their way through many tournaments over the last decade or so. Today, flippin' is popular with tournament anglers and amateurs alike.

Suk used a Quantum 7½-foot XL Flippin' Stick, but recently switched to the Tour Edition because of its additional sensitivity. His Quantum Pitchin' & Flippin' reel basically does nothing but hold extra line. As a rule, 12 to 15 feet is the length that works best for Suk.

"If I let out too much line," he says, "my accuracy suffers. Catching fish depends upon dropping the lure exactly where I want it, and that's frequently into an opening no more than a few inches around." Suk smiles and adds, "In fact, sometimes I wonder how I would ever get a fish out of some of these places if I did hook one."

Suk regularly flips with a jig-and-pig but has recently started using 3-inch Good Ol' Weenies Grubs (made in Mesa, Arizona).

He first started with large grubs made by Kalin or Gary Yamamoto but soon discovered that the smaller ones seemed to catch more fish in clearwater lakes. Using a smaller lure is the only adjustment he makes in regard to water clarity, however.

Havasu's tule haven is not the only water where Suk's flippin' has paid off. "While many of the lakes with clear water lack green vegetation, a few do have lots of flooded salt cedars that have been there for years. And when the water rises (which is normal for these reservoirs in spring), it floods more trees. Flippin' works just as well in the trees as it does in the tules."

When he gets on a clear lake without any vegetation, Suk changes to split-shotting or fishing with a Carolina rig. "I usually look for structure that offers good cover," he says, "whether it's big rocks or a steep cliff with undercuts and ledges. Largemouth bass love to ambush their victims, so I look for likely places they can find to do this.

"If the fish are hiding among the rocks in shallow water, I flip them because a split shot or Carolina rig makes a splash that can spook them. If they are in deeper water, I use the other methods. Basically, it means adjusting to the season, weather and the time of day."

For summertime fishing, Suk tries to find the food bass are feeding on. If they are gorging on crayfish, he fishes the lake's rocky areas and where the bottom is fairly hard. If bass are feeding on shad, he usually concentrates on underwater structure and outside points.

"It depends upon the time of day," he says. "Bass frequently move into shallow water to feed early and late in the day. So that's where I fish for them. As the sun gets higher and more light penetrates the water, they move deeper, and so do I."

Later in the year, Suk moves into the coves where bass regularly pursue congregated shad.

"If the fish are in shallow water," he says, "I'll normally change to a light spinning rig and 6-pound line to throw crankbaits or small, in-line spinners like a Mepps, Vibrex or Panther Martin. I also throw a spinnerbait, usually with a white or chartreuse skirt, with casting tackle.

"Then as the temperatures start to drop in late fall, bass start hanging around steeper points and sharp-dropping walls. The drop-offs along river channels can be productive. I'll often cruise

Suk looks for schools of shad in the shallower water, and the bass usually will be nearby. If the fish are shallow, he'll switch to a light spinning rig and 6-pound-test line.

this area real slow and watch my graph. If I see large schools of shad, I start fishing. If the water depth is 15 feet or less, I'll usually split-shot. In deeper water, though, I'll use the Carolina rig, mostly because it gets down quicker," he says.

Suk's Carolina rig consists of a slip sinker, large bead, barrel swivel and hook. He first slides the slip sinker and bead onto the line, then ties on the barrel swivel. Next he ties an 18- to 36-inch leader to the other swivel loop. (The hook goes on the end of this leader.) The bead's purpose is to make noise as it wedges between the slip sinker and swivel.

"I usually start with a long leader and cut it back if necessary," he says. "Because I always use a floating plastic bait on the Carolina setup, the length of the leader regulates the distance the lure rises off the bottom. Naturally, the ideal distance is the one where the fish are holding. Although your graph can help determine this, actually catching fish is the only way to be sure. Once you know that depth, the rest is easy." Suk also adjusts the depth of his lure with his split-shotting technique in much the same way. Instead of changing leader length, however, he merely moves his split-shot weights farther up the line.

Solving The Clearwater Mystery

I fished with Suk on Arizona's Apache Lake last December. The water is a bit murkier than the lakes on the Colorado River, but it harbors a good population of smallmouth bass. Although we were going more specifically for largemouth, we knew the odds of hooking into a smallmouth were good, also. Suk had already mapped his strategy. Because it had been cold for several days, he expected the fish would be staying on the flats and points closest to the main river channel.

We headed to a spot where Suk had caught about a dozen largemouths and smallmouths the previous week. "The fish were all concentrated in one area along the right side of the river channel," Suk explained. "I first picked them up on the graph in about 12 feet of water, but they were schooled all the way into the deeper areas, too. There were also lots of shad in the area. I first tried a deep-running, shad-type crankbait on a casting rod and caught one small largemouth in an hour. As that's not my idea of an exciting day, I decided to switch to split-shotting.

"I started off with a Good Ol' Weenies Grub, and it didn't do any better than the crankbait. In fact, I never hooked a fish even though I got a few half-hearted hits. The annoying thing was that I knew the fish were there; they just weren't biting well for some reason. So I decided to go to lighter line and a smaller lure.

"I tied on a Good Ol' Grub that is supposed to mimic a shad," he continued. "It's salt-and-pepper with a chartreuse tail. A 2-pound largemouth picked it up on the second cast, and I managed to catch a bunch more over the next couple of hours. I even caught two smallmouths in the same spot. To this day, I think using the lighter line in that clear water did the trick, even though the smaller lure might have been partially responsible."

When we reached the place Suk wanted to fish, he slowed the boat and slowly headed out from the shallow water toward the middle of the lake. In his hand, he held a marker buoy. When the graph showed what he was looking for, he dropped the buoy over the side. Then he repeated the same maneuver about 50 feet up the lake.

"That's the edge of the channel," he said. "We'll fish about 10 feet to the side of it. The graph already picked up some fish there." He tossed me a grub. "Tie that on."

It was salt-and-pepper with a chartreuse tail. "So this is the secret lure?" I asked.

"You got it," he said. "By the way, what weight line do you have?"

I had 14-pound Trilene on a medium-weight Berkley Lightning casting rod with a Daiwa levelwind on it. Suk smiled as he handed me a few split shot. "Well, you can try it," he said, "but I have a feeling you'll want to use one of my rods pretty quick. Pinch one on about 18 inches up the line."

We cast onto the flat and pulled the grubs to the drop-off. Five fish were hooked over the next 30 minutes. Unfortunately, none were mine. Suk handed me a rigged setup identical to his. "Here," he said. "Wanna bet you catch fish with this? Hang one of those grubs on it."

Within 10 minutes of my first cast, I caught a hefty smallmouth. Minutes later, I hooked my first largemouth of the day. The only major difference between my gear and Suk's was the line—he had 6-pound test. Then, suddenly, the fish quit biting.

Using the trolling motor, Suk moved the boat about 20 yards into the channel. "The fish moved off the shelf as the sun got higher," he said. "In this clear water, the light can really bother them. My guess would be they are now in the deeper water right in the channel."

His hunch was right again. Now, instead of casting far up on the flat, we simply made sure we hit it. Then we pulled the grub to the drop-off and let it slowly sink. It was just another part of the equation that Suk uses to catch fish on clearwater lakes.

3

Proven Techniques For Small-Water Bass

by Larry Larsen

Dave Hoy let out a yelp as he set the hook into a 2-pound bass. The fish flew out of the water beside the cattails and was grabbed by the guide in midair. Ten feet farther along the dense cover's edge, the central Florida guide hooked up with another, larger bass. He quickly hauled the 4-pounder over the gunwale and continued his short-line method along the cattails. Hoy flipped his worms into the weeds, methodically working the pockets and holes. A few flips later, the angler was straining to control a heavier fish. Hoy's stiff rod bent double as the largemouth bulled into the dense habitat.

Forcing the bass to the surface, Hoy tried swinging it into the boat with one motion. The attempt failed as the fish bounced off the side. Hoy quickly knelt and grabbed the lip of the 10-pounder as it wallowed on the surface. He firmly swung it aboard, and after a few pictures, relieved the bass of the 4/0 worm hook. He carefully placed the giant back in the water and watched it slowly swim into the depths.

Flippin' is a deadly method—and one of Hoy's favorites—for catching bass on small, highly vegetated waters. Such tactics are perfect for tiny environments—places where the quiet approach is often best. A worm, flipped around masses of vegetation that cover most every foot of a small lake's perimeter, is very effective.

The guide worked his Texas-rigged worm into and out of several holes in the dense stands of cattails. His 7-foot rod and well-practiced swing-cast dropped the bait into small openings in the

Guide Dave Hoy's favorite spot for finding bass in small waters is anywhere there is a mixture of hydrilla and other underwater vegetation. He usually will use a jerk-type bait.

Proven Techniques For Small-Water Bass

vegetation. Within an hour, he had covered all of the shallow-water habitat. Hoy had caught and released a dozen bass, including the big female and another weighing about 6 pounds.

Hoy and his Professional Bass Guide Service clients often fish man-made waters around his Florida base. Phosphate pits, barrow pits and other tiny impoundments are what attracts this bass guide. Bass up to 14 pounds have been taken by Hoy and his clients in the small waters he regularly fishes. Sometimes, though, the fishing can run hot one day and cold the next.

Few small waters are highly pressured. This is because a vast number of these fisheries (near most anglers) are often overlooked. Anglers tend to fish larger, better-known public waters. Thousands of these tiny impoundments exist in most states. Many are on private lands, others are fee-ponds, but still others are open to public use.

Ponds created in conjunction with highway projects, strip mining and building developments are generally open to the public. Pits may be from one acre to 500 or so, and the terrain is equally varied. Some have vast pad beds; others have cattails and bulrushes. And, sometimes they are nearly void of emergent vegetation. Depth in man-made waters also varies from site to site, but many are 40 feet deep or more.

When massive earth-moving buckets are dug through the soil to the rock beneath, they create dead-end channels, island rows and structure and depth variations. The small pits contain humps, deep holes and even mountains—places that Hoy utilizes to catch thousands of bass. Hoy locates bass action that is hard to surpass over the irregular bottom topography.

Feeding Influences

Weather doesn't seem to affect the bass in man-made waters as much as it does in natural waters, according to Hoy. Bass normally retreat to the deeper waters and remain feeding actively during hot summer months. When depths average 10 to 25 feet, the water temperatures are usually very comfortable.

"In the deeper waters, the temperature may vary from year to year and month to month," says Hoy, "but it is usually higher in the winter and cooler in the summer than in shallower waters."

Water color and clarity affect the temperature of man-made waters, though. The color varies from place to place, and many

Fishing Small Man-Made Waters

Fishing submerged bars in the open-water areas of small man-made waters often provides maximum action. As shown here, find a drop and use a deep-running crankbait to dig into the structure during the retrieve.

waters are stained a "tea" color. Water clarity depends upon shoreline characteristics, drainage land and degree of water manipulation (if any); however, most such waters have visibility of about 2 feet or more.

Many small waters are forage-intensive because of abundant nutrients in the soil and runoff. A large food base usually results in a good fishery for largemouth bass. In fact, one of Hoy's key strategies in locating bass in the small waters is knowing the predominant forage and its location.

Basing the lure selection on the predominant forage is a wise idea, the guide believes. Both shad and shiners are often abundant in man-made waters. Shiners prefer those waters that are vegetated and they normally inhabit the shallows at depths of 2 to 10 feet. Shad schools normally roam the open waters of the slightly larger ponds.

Bar Hopping

The small-water specialist recommends fishing any submerged bars in the open-water areas of a man-made lake for maximum action. Anchor over a drop-off and fish a plastic worm slowly, or use

Working Small Natural Ponds

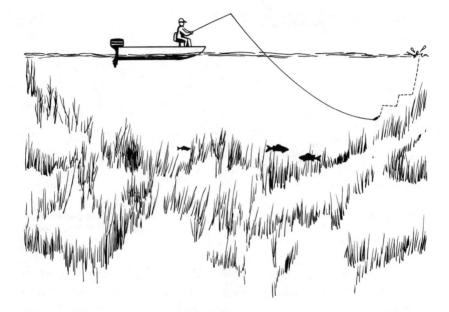

A productive technique for small, natural ponds with highly vegetated lake bottom is to "yo-yo" vibrating plugs. Use this on schools of bass buried in grass on the lake's bottom.

a deep-running crankbait during the summer months. A lot of big bass swim in these waters.

Another productive technique for Hoy has been "yo-yoing" vibrating plugs over highly vegetated lake bottoms. He has used such tactics on schools of bass which he located in the depths with sonar. He'll watch as his electronics cover the bottom, because that is usually the key to locating bass. Find the drops and other structure on or near the bottom, and you'll find fish.

Bass in small, clearwater ponds relate to depth, according to the guide. Any "roughage" along the bottom, such as rock, brush or submerged grass, will concentrate the fish. Like many bass populations, those in the man-dug waters are somewhat fragile, so efforts to maintain a quality fishery are usually necessary. Such bass can be easily cleaned out by just a few greedy anglers, so Hoy believes strongly in releasing the majority of the bass to ensure their future and continued angler success. The irregular bottom of many small waters can concentrate bass long after the shore-bound populations have dwindled to practically nothing.

Hoy has often located ridges with submerged rock piles in 10 to 15 feet of water and concentrations of hungry bass around the bottom structure. On several occasions, he has had two, three or four consecutive strikes on the same number of casts. Such action over the years has afforded him the opportunity to catch and release thousands of bass. Small waters often contain larger-sized bass populations on the average than larger lakes, and they can contain monsters. While many tiny waters have trophy-sized bass, others may have numerous smaller fish.

Lure Tactics

On most small waters, Hoy finds that casting rushes and cat-tails early, then moving against them to flip plastic worms is often productive for all sizes of largemouth. Moving farther inside the cattails and flippin' the really dense stuff is sometimes necessary in the summer heat. Black with chartreuse tail, moccasin, blueberry and red shad are prime color combinations for the flippin'-worm fare on most small waters, according to Hoy.

Most silver and/or white plugs imitating shad or shiners will attract small-water largemouth, according to Hoy. Shad-imitation crankbaits worked along the cover's edges and over irregular bot-toms in open water are proven producers. Hoy also recommends using them near the surface.

"The shad or shiner imitator can be cranked through schools of surface-feeding baitfish to attract bass from below," he ex-plains. "Such a tactic may be effective when the crankbait is fished beneath a ball of forage. Bass will be positioned below them ready to strike out at a bait that swims away from that ball."

Plastic crayfish are also effective in man-dug waters. Such im-itations work particularly well on bass which are relating to changes in bottom structure. Rock piles and submerged brush of-ten harbor big bass, and they can be fooled by a rubber lure. Hoy likes to toss Texas-rigged plastic baits and bounce them along un-even terrain. That will usually result in strikes.

Snakes, eels and crayfish are all abundant in most small wa-ters, so it is wise to keep your eyes peeled for signs of such species.

Hoy maintains an assortment of crankbaits of many different colors. He has found that matching a crankbait with the predominant forage is a great producer.

Complete Angler's Library

Here Hoy used a weedless bait for fishing the dense cover that small ponds usually offer in great abundance.

Then you can select the lure accordingly.

Natural Ponds

Many natural lakes that Hoy fishes have perimeter cattails and bulrushes. The clear, tea-colored water of many of these small lakes engulfs cattails, trees, grasses and other aquatic vegetation. Some have lily pads, pencil rushes and other vegetation that produce well.

Many natural ponds average 10 to 12 feet in depth and are lined with cattails and grass beds. The lakes Hoy prefers range from a few acres to 250 or more. Some are surrounded by residential areas or office parks in a few cases; however, most have some natural topography existing along some of the shorelines. A few on the edges of various towns adjoin citrus groves or farmland.

Hoy suggests tossing Texas-rigged worms with "pegged" slip sinkers. A toothpick is inserted into the weight hole beside the line, and its point is broken off. This wedges the sinker to the line and prevents it from sliding up and down, resulting in better control of the rig as it's placed in a pothole beside the rush stalks, jigged up and down, and then moved to another opening. Get the bait into the densest cover for maximum action, Hoy says.

While flippin' is very effective, so is swimming a plastic worm

Don't be afraid to use plastic worms for another tantalizing, weedless bait for bass that are holding in dense cover.

or spoon through the pad vegetation in 3 to 6 feet of water. Spinnerbaits and weedless spoons are also effective on vegetated waters. Fish a willow-leaf blade spinnerbait, or a spoon with grub trailer, in any emergent plant beds for best results. Tossing a tiny topwater plug will also fool a bass or two about any time of the year. Hoy recommends a ¼ or ½-ounce bill-less crankbait for working those areas adjacent to vegetation.

Fishing any offshore vegetation, whether emergent or submerged, in particular, can be productive on the small, natural waters. Some of Hoy's favorite spots in highly vegetated ponds are where reeds are mixed with cattail patches. Hydrilla and other underwater vegetation mixed in with reeds or other tall, emergent plants are places he searches by tossing a topwater, jerk-type bait or stick-type bait.

"Fish in relatively clear water are basically sight feeders," he says. "The lighter-weight worm rigs, like the Carolina rig, can be very productive over short grass patches. Areas where the grass mixes with hydrilla or isolated reed patches are where the bass gang up."

To catch bass from canals that lie off many small waters, Hoy suggests fishing them early in the day with a topwater plug or shallow-running crankbait. Worms with light bullet weights are effective when flipped against the vegetation growing off the canal edges. The seawall structure found along some canals are good locations for finding bedding bass.

"Big bass want to bed up against something," explains the guide. "A sand bottom over most of a small lake or pond provides excellent spawning grounds."

When fishing shallow waters in a canal or a small, very clear lake, it is wise to use light line and make long casts to avoid spooking the fish. Monofilament testing 8 to 12 pounds is Hoy's favorite when dealing with such clarity. Light lures complete the balanced rig. Spring is topwater time, with active bass in a small canal or pond drawn to almost any topwater activity.

Drift-Fishing

After midmorning, bass in small, clear ponds often move deeper or tighter to cover. Then dragging a plastic worm along drop-offs can be effective. Once you have located a drop of only a foot or even 6 inches, drag the worm with ¼-ounce weight along the bottom. To slow the drift in high winds, Hoy drags a water parachute or a 5-gallon bucket.

"Letting the wind push you through an area is one of the best ways to fish," he says. "In a small pond, you can cover a large area on a drift and pick up a lot of bass away from the shore. If you drift through an area and get a bite or catch a fish, throw out a marker and continue making passes. You'll need the marker, even in small waters, to have something on which to line up the drifts."

Another bait, effective in deeper, offshore areas of a small pond or pit, is the live shiner. In fact, if your target is trophy bass, a live shiner is the best. Pull a golden shiner across an underwater grass bed or float one against a reed point and hang onto the rod.

Small waters often have dry creekbeds or ravines running into them. They normally play a small role in Hoy's small-water strategy, unless water is flowing through them. After heavy rains, for example, tiny creeks and their mouths become contact points for bass congregations, but the great runoff fishing on small waters won't last long. When the flow has stopped, the bass scatter, and the previous patterns are no longer valid.

Reading Small Waters

If you don't have sonar, you'll have to eyeball the terrain

Hoy believes that small boats and small waters go together. He's found that these smaller waters can be worked best with a smaller boat.

above water and try to analyze it. Successful pothole angling can be accomplished by learning to "read the water." Fortunately, it is easier to read small waters like man-dug pits.

"If you can't chart the bottom," Hoy says, "you'll have to figure out the lay of the land. Many topographical variations will cry out for your casts, yet some are not as productive as others.

"For example, portions of a pit that have been more recently dug usually have less brush or other mature growth beneath the water's surface," he continues. "Recently created islands with minimal erosion and vegetated growth are less inviting to forage and, correspondingly, to bass."

However, rows of islands in man-made ponds or pits can often be deceiving. The best areas may be the submerged portions left behind in the strip mining operation. The "saddles" between the outcroppings are often great areas for largemouth concentrations.

"Likewise, you'll want to try the points and extensions to the rows of islands," Hoy adds. "If the bass are not in the shallower 3 to 8 feet of water, move and cast to deeper spots."

Many of Hoy's small-water honeyholes are not obvious. He tries to find bass concentrations away from the shoreline, so if

Complete Angler's Library

there are other anglers, he has a chance of keeping that spot to himself.

Most small waters with excellent bass angling are fished primarily by local anglers. Little waters generate little talk or publicity. Hundreds of these small-water angling opportunities exist around the country. Many are open to public fishing or to anglers requesting permission to wet a line.

For many small lakes, there are paved roads to their shores, while some may only be reached by those with a small cartopper boat transported down a dirt or gravel road. Ramps, made of dirt or concrete, vary widely in condition.

The largemouth in small waters can range in size from less than a pound to more than 10, so Hoy suggests using the proper tackle. It should be sized according to what you might expect to find. Huge bass are a reality in some small waters, so stout tackle may be required. Medium-heavy action rods and good quality reels spooled with 14- or 17-pound-test line should provide adequate insurance for landing that once-in-a-lifetime bass.

4

Canadian Shield Smallmouth

by Gary Clancy

During nine months each year, Gary Nordlie stands in the front of his classroom and teaches English to his students, a job he has done, and done well for 24 years. But for the other three months—June, July and August—Nordlie conducts class from the deck of his favorite classroom: a 16-foot, deep-v, fishing machine.

Operating out of his summer cabin on Lake Vermillion, one of the many lakes straddling the Minnesota and Ontario border, Nordlie guides anglers on his home lake, as well as Kabetogama, Namakan, Crane and Lac La Croix lakes. (All are "big names" within the smallmouth crowd.) He also takes his clients to smaller lakes, most of which can only be reached by canoe.

These waters are commonly known as Canadian Shield lakes or simply shield lakes. Shield lakes were created over 10,000 years ago when glaciers slowly retreated to the north, moving ponderously but powerfully over the land. Glaciers scraped away the soil right down to the bedrock, leaving behind thousands of deep, cold, infertile lakes. Shield lakes in the far north are home to mainly lake trout and northern pike. However, lakes in the shield's southern end support various fish, often lake trout in the deep water and walleyes, northern pike and smallmouth bass in shallower waters. This story is about the smallmouth.

Rocks, Rocks And More Rocks

"You hear people say all the time that smallmouth bass are

Trash fish? Local anglers around the Canadian Shield lakes may consider these smallmouth bass to be trash, but guide Gary Nordlie is showing his clients that these bass are fine gamefish.

Canadian Shield Smallmouth

easy to find," Nordlie says, "because all you have to do is look for the rocks. Find the rocks, they say, and you will find the smallmouth. Well, those anglers must not ever have fished up here on a shield lake. These lakes *are* rock. The trick to catching them is eliminating the 95 percent of the rock which does not hold fish and concentrating on the 5 percent which does.

"Most of the rock on these lakes is what I call slab rock. Big slabs of unbroken, mostly smooth rock," he continues. "There are few places for a smallmouth to hide in slab rock, so you won't find many fish around them. What I look for is broken-up rock— places where the huge slabs have broken into many smaller slabs. Usually these smaller slabs will be stacked at crazy angles where they fell after breaking off from the huge slabs. Smallies love to hide in the shade of these smaller slabs, feeding mostly on the crayfish which also call the nooks and crannies home.

"The next stage is when you find a stretch of shoreline where the rocks have broken down into small boulders and rubble. All shield lakes are different, and some have enough of these areas that force you to seek out the very best to find the fish. But on most shield lakes, these areas are at a premium, and when you do locate them, you will also find fish," he says.

Fish will be there because those areas offer the fish everything it needs to survive. The larger boulders offer the smallmouth shade when the summer sun is high overhead. The rubble is home to crayfish, minnows and varied insect life—the three staples of the smallmouth's diet. These places have it all.

Weeds

"Weeds don't grow on rock, so shield lakes don't have many weeds," says Nordlie. "But, here and there, you will find a sand bottom. If this is the case, you will often find some vegetation. If the sand is close to shore, most often the vegetation will be bulrushes, which you can see sticking up like green spears above the surface. Or, it will be celery which grows under the surface. In deeper water, you might find an isolated cabbage bed. All three types will attract and hold smallmouth bass.

"Always watch the shoreline," he continues. "If the rocky shoreline suddenly turns into a sand beach, it is a good bet that the underwater composition is the same. Check it out. If you find weeds, fish them. But even if you don't find weeds, always fish the

Weeds like these are a rarity in most shield lakes; however, when you find them, you have an excellent chance of finding smallmouth.

seam where the rocks peter out to sand; there will nearly always be smallmouth holding along that edge.

"Many anglers make the mistake of fishing only the outside edge of these shoreline weeds. Often, smallmouth will hold on the inside edge. You need to toss your lure or bait right up on shore and then slowly work it out to the weeds," he says.

Cabbage beds are a magnet for smallmouth bass. Late in the summer, cabbage grows right on the surface. (On a calm day, you can spot it by the tassels poking just above the surface.) If there is just enough breeze to ripple the water, look for spots where the water is mysteriously calm. Usually you will find a cabbage bed. Early in the season, however, cabbage is more difficult to locate. Sometimes you find it by accident, casting or trolling, when you hang up on a stalk. Don't just cuss the snag and move on; fish the

Locating Smallmouths In The Shallows

Smallmouth often will hold between the weeds and the shoreline. This illustration shows where to put your lure. It's a spot that you don't want to overlook.

area thoroughly. It is most likely a home for smallies. You can also spot the beds on your locator. "Whenever you find weeds," Nordlie says, "mark the spot on your map. You can come back time after time and catch smallies from these locations."

Up Close And Personal

The most exciting smallmouth bass fishing occurs when the fish are shallow. Fish in shallow water are more likely to take a topwater bait than fish in deep water. The ultimate in smallmouth fishing is to have a husky smallie shatter the silence by smacking a topwater lure. Fly-rod enthusiasts live for a big bronzeback engulfing their carefully presented deerhair bug.

"How long the fish stay in shallow water depends more on the lake than the time of year," says Nordlie. "Many of the shield lakes are fed by streams which course through tamarack bogs. The water is bog-stained a tea-brown color. Because the dark water prevents sunlight from penetrating very deep, smallies in these lakes can stay shallow all summer. However, the best shallow-water action occurs from the opener until sometime in early July. By that time, even though there will still be small fish in the shallows, most of the better fish have moved into deeper water.

"I like to cruise along the shoreline," Nordlie says, "using my electric motor to stay a long cast away from my target so that I don't spook the fish. Then I cast to those areas which look like they should hold fish—places with broken rocks, boulder slides, the seam where sand meets rock or weedbeds. Other locations you never want to pass without throwing a lure are fallen trees and crib docks. Wearing polarized sunglasses helps cut glare so you can see what the structure looks like underwater. Sometimes you can even spot the fish.

"Trees can't get much of a root system established in the thin, shield soil, so they are always being pushed over by the wind," he continues. "Wherever a tree has fallen into the water, there is a good chance that a smallie has set up housekeeping in its branches. I've caught a half dozen smallies from under one tree on many occasions. Never pass them by."

Another overlooked hotspot are dock cribs, a pyramid of rocks of different sizes on which the docks rest. Crayfish are numerous in the crib's many crevices, and smallmouth bass move in to feast on this prey. One tip for fishing dock cribs: The biggest smallmouths will be on the crib's shady side.

Techniques For Shallow Smallies

Floating Rapalas and the Jitterbug are Nordlie's one-two punch for shallow-water bass. He fishes them on the same rig he uses for all his smallmouth fishing, a lightweight Fenwick 6½-foot, graphite spinning rod and a spinning reel loaded with 6-pound-test line.

"Smallies can be fussy when it comes to the action they want," says Nordlie. "One day, they want the lure brought back on a steady retrieve. The next day, you can let the lure lay where it lands until the rings have all disappeared and then give it a little twitch. I've given up trying to outguess them; I just let them make the decision for me, and then I give them what they want."

Surface plugs work best when the water is calm. If the water is rippled or the surface plugs don't entice the fish, Nordlie switches to live bait.

"Sure, you can catch smallmouth bass on crankbaits and spinnerbaits when they won't hit on the surface," he says, "but I've found that nothing beats live bait when the fish are feeding below the surface. Besides, those lures are expensive, and these rocks will just eat 'em up. When I snag up using live bait, all I'm going to lose is a hook and sinker or maybe a jighead. Knowing that, I'm more likely to go ahead and toss my bait into places where a snag is likely. More often than not, those are the same places the fish hang out."

Two techniques work best for Nordlie. He fishes a 3-inch Mister Twister tail on a 1/16-ounce jighead and tips it with a leech or piece of crawler. It takes some time to develop the touch you need to keep the jig swimming just over the rocks. Most anglers get discouraged after hanging up several times and quit. But if you stay with it, you will develop the "touch," and then you have the most dependable fish-catching technique always at your disposal. Nothing beats a jig. Even when fished without bait, a jig resembles everything a smallie feeds on naturally. Learn to fish a jig, and you can nearly always catch smallies.

The second technique is slip-bobber fishing. A lot of Nordlie's customers are not avid anglers; they really are not interested in learning to fish a jig. All they want to do is have a good time and catch a bunch of fish without the hassle of being snagged all the time. The slip bobber is the answer. Adjust the bobber stop so the bait (usually a leech) dangles about a foot above bottom. A hook, split shot, bobber and slipknot—what could be easier?

Deep-Water Smallmouth

While some smallmouth bass may remain in the shallows longer than normal, or possibly throughout the year, most of them will move out to deeper water around mid-July. So this is when you have to be innovative as a bass angler because where they move depends upon what is available. The following two scenarios are commonly found on these lakes:

Shield lakes are studded with points. Smallmouth bass that spent the spring and early summer in shallow water at the point's base will slip out into deeper water (usually in the 15-foot range).

Some mid-lake reefs top out just above the surface of the water so they are easy to spot. Most reefs, however, are under the surface and can be found only with your depthfinder.

Remembering the shallow points holding bass in early summer will pay big dividends later when the fish move deeper. The best points are those with slow-tapering sides and a rubble-and-rocks mixture big enough to give the fish shade. Add a cabbage bed and you have smallmouth heaven.

Smallmouth bass which inhabited straight sections of shallows along the shoreline will sometimes move off the shoreline into deeper water, especially if the drop-off is very gradual. But often these fish end up on reefs. Common on shield lakes, reefs account for many nicked propellers and damaged lower units. The best reefs for smallmouth bass are 3 to 12 feet deep.

"All of these lakes are loaded with reefs, and most of them never get touched," says Nordlie. "Fishermen concentrate on the bigger, better-known reefs. Well sure, big reefs attract more fish,

Reefs that are submerged off of small islands like the one in the background often receive little fishing pressure, and often are home to fair numbers of fish.

but I figure if most of them get caught they aren't doing me much good. I like to fish the smaller reefs. They might only give up three or four fish, but there are hundreds of small reefs to fish.

"The first thing I do is throw a crankbait up on top of the reef," he continues. "A couple of casts will tell me if there are fish right up on top or not. If the fish are on top, I stash the crankbait and go to work on them with live bait. If there are no fish on top, I run the sides of the reef, watching my locator for signs of fish. Walleyes and smallmouth share most reefs, with the walleyes usually being deeper. I commonly spot the smallmouth in 15 feet of water and the walleyes down in the 30-foot range. Once I've spotted them, I park right on them and feed them live bait for as long as they will take it.

"Most of the time I'll go with the jig, but sometimes a Lindy

Rig will work better, especially if the water is rough.

"My favorite live bait in the summer is nightcrawlers, but I use more leeches than crawlers because the leeches are tougher and aren't picked off as easy by perch. Leeches are easier to keep alive, too. Minnows get the nod if I can't get leeches or crawlers."

Electronics are necessary when fishing these reefs. It doesn't matter if you use a flasher, LCD or paper graph as long as you take time to observe each reef's sides, and then believe what the unit tells you. You won't always catch those fish, but it sure beats fishing blind. If they're not biting, try them later.

Up A Creek

Shield lakes are fed by streams and rivers. Smallmouth bass love moving water; yet, the rivers which connect or empty into

Best Areas For River Smallies

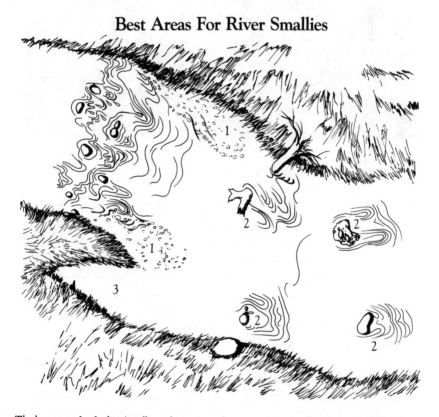

The best spots for finding smallmouths in rivers that empty into the shield lakes are: (1) below foam in eddies, (2) behind rocks or other obstructions and (3) in quiet water of side bays.

Mouths of rivers are a good spot for finding shield smallmouths such as being done here. Notice the flecks of foam on the water in the foreground.

shield lakes are virtually ignored by smallmouth anglers. By carefully maneuvering your boat up river as far as you can, which is usually as far as the first set of rapids, you can often treat yourself to some fantastic and untouched smallmouth fishing.

"When fishing the rivers, I rely on an in-line spinner like a Mepps," says Nordlie. "Rivers will really gobble up the tackle, but spinners seem to hang up less than anything I've tried and they really catch fish. And let me tell you, when you hang a good smallie in the river, you have got your hands full.

"Smallies can handle a lot of current, but you will catch the most fish by bringing that spinner through places where the current is cut by some obstruction, usually a big rock. Another place that always holds a bunch of fish is where an eddy forms below rapids. Most of the time these eddies will be topped by a big head of white foam, just like a mug of beer. Toss your spinner right into the foam. The smallies lay under the foam where, I suppose, they get out of the main current and enjoy the foam's shade.

"River smallies can save the trip when a cold front shuts down the action on the lake. I don't know why, but river fish are much less affected by a cold front than lake fish," he says.

Tow A Canoe

Some of the best smallmouth bass fishing in the world is in the canoe country of the Minnesota-Ontario Boundary Waters Canoe Area and Quetico Provincial Park wilderness. But even when fishing the big shield lakes, like Vermillion, Kabetogama, Crane and Namakan, savvy anglers often tow a canoe. Several dozen small lakes can be reached by portage from the bigger lakes. Many of these lakes are loaded with smallmouth bass which receive very little fishing pressure.

"Most people up here are walleye crazy," says Nordlie. "The walleye is the glamour fish. Few people fish seriously for smallmouth. In fact, many of the locals still look upon the smallmouth as some kind of trash fish. So naturally, even the lakes which are easily accessible don't receive a lot of pressure on the smallmouth. Those that require some effort to reach hardly get touched.

"The ultimate smallmouth trip is to take your family or some friends and rent a houseboat," he concludes. "Behind the houseboat you can tow your fishing boat and a couple of canoes. Every evening you can dock the houseboat in a different location and spend the days fishing for smallmouth, always checking new water. When you feel like it, you can take the canoes, make a short portage back into one of these lakes and spend the day catching smallmouths until your arms literally ache. Then it's back to the houseboat for a roaring campfire, hot shower and some golden crisp fillets. The next morning, you get up and do it all over again. Now that is what I call living!"

Panfish

5

Jigging Spoons
For Crappies

by John Phillips

fter the spawn, most crappie fishermen usually shift their attention to other species or seek the comfort of their air-conditioned homes. If they do venture out later to take papermouths, they may fish only after dark when the air and water temperatures are lower, and the slabs can be attracted to light. Summertime crappie fishermen usually adhere to one of three philosophies:

● Crappies do not bite during daylight hours in the hot summer months.

● Crappies cannot be found during daylight hours because they crawl into holes in lake bottoms.

● Anglers cannot find and take enough crappies during daylight in the summertime to make fishing for crappies worth the time and effort.

These beliefs allow anglers who know how to find reservoir crappies during summer to locate and catch more crappies than they could if most crappie anglers understood the secrets of hot-weather crappie fishing.

When air temperature increases and frying an egg on the sidewalk becomes a distinct possibility, most crappies will be in deep water, searching for the cooler thermocline. During this time of year when crappies are biting slowly and water-surface temperatures in the South may hit 90-plus degrees, Charlie Ingram from Eufaula, Alabama, uses a bass technique and tackle to put more papermouths in his boat. Ingram's fishing system produces

Charlie Ingram has discovered the secret for taking crappies during the midsummer doldrums by using a technique usually associated with bass—the jigging spoon.

Jigging Spoons For Crappies   55

crappies on any lake in the nation in torrid weather.

"Remember, crappies must eat all year long," Ingram says. "All you have to do to catch crappies at any time of the year on any lake is find and present a bait to them that they'll take.

"Successful crappie fishing involves understanding that crappie angling is not that much different from bass fishing. Both crappies and bass have seasonal migration patterns, hold in heavy cover and move into creek and river channels in summer months. I noticed when I'd be exploring old creek and river channels with my depthfinder in the summertime for spots to catch bass that I would often see large schools of crappies. I knew these schools were crappies because they appeared larger on the screen than baitfish. Also, when I cast a plastic worm or a deep-diving crankbait to these fish, they wouldn't hit either lure. Sometimes these schools of fish were holding in brush and cover on deep creek channels and river ledges in the same locations where the bass were," he says.

Ingram is primarily a spoon fisherman when bass are deep during summer. He has found that the 3/4-ounce Jack Chancellor and Hopkins jigging spoon are the deadliest lures available for catching bass in deep water.

"But when I let my jigging spoon down into the cover on these river and creek channels," Ingram says, "for every bass I caught, I took five to 10 crappies—big ones, too. I realized any crappie that could inhale a 3/4-ounce jigging spoon usually had to be larger than 1/2 pound in size."

When bass fishing was slow in the summer, he would take only six to 10 bass and a mere one or two bass on a bad day. On any given day, however, he would catch 30 to 50 crappies.

A transformation came over Charlie Ingram, the bass angler, as he experimented with his jigging spoon during the summer.

"I found I had more fun catching crappies than I did bass," Ingram says. "My family and friends enjoyed eating the crappies I caught. Using this system of jigging, I could release all the bass I took every day and still go home with a mess of crappies for the skillet."

To catch more crappies and still not lose the bass that attacked the spoon, Ingram modified the hooks on his jigging spoons.

Ingram says the hooks on the jigging spoon are so sharp they'll tear the mouths of crappies when you're working them through

Ingram catches crappies with their paper-thin mouths using a jigging spoon and treble hook. He dulls the points on the hook so it won't rip out of the fish's mouth.

cover. He adds, "I've learned a sharp hook gets hung in the cover much easier than a dull one, so I take a file and lightly pass it over the tips of each one of the treble hooks. By dulling the hooks, I can fish the jigging spoon through the thickest cover and not lose a spoon all day long."

You don't have to set the hook hard on a crappie or a bass when utilizing this technique. If you touch a limb, jiggle the spoon. The bait's weight will make it come free easily if the hooks are somewhat dull.

We've all been taught that sharp hooks catch more bass than dull hooks. It would seem, therefore, that Ingram is limiting his effectiveness for fishing bass by using dull hooks to catch crappies. However, as Ingram explains, "I've learned when a bass hits a jigging spoon in the summertime, it inhales the lure. Ninety percent of the bass I catch with the jigging spoon will have the spoon either in their throats or deep in their mouths. I rarely lip-hook a bass or a crappie when fishing the jigging spoon in hot weather."

Ingram hooks most fish deep in the mouth because of the action he gives the jigging spoon. Most anglers would fish the jigging spoon by lowering the bait to the bottom, making three or four hard twitches toward the surface and then letting the spoon fall back to the bottom. Also, because the spoon is such a heavy bait, most anglers don't fish it until the fall.

But Ingram lowers the bait down to the cover, gently raises his rodtip up 6 inches, and then lowers it again 6 inches. This slow, up-and-down movement is used from 6 feet below the surface down to the cover including submerged bushes and treetops, through the cover and down to the bottom. Once the lure hits bottom, Ingram uses this slow, up-and-down movement to work the lure back to the surface.

"Keep in mind that during the summer months when the weather is hot and the fish are deep, crappies most likely will not be aggressive," Ingram says. "They don't want to chase lures. However, if you bounce baits off their noses, they will inhale the lures. Crappies especially are not going to come out of cover and pursue baits like they will in the spring. They'll be holding in thick cover and waiting on minnows and shad they can ambush easily.

"When a jigging spoon drops into cover where both bass and crappies are holding and starts to rise and fall slowly," he continues, "either the bass or the crappie or both will inhale the spoon. The action I use resembles taking a teaspoon, slowly putting it all the way down to the bottom of a tall, iced-tea glass and then slowly pulling the spoon all the way out of the glass. Most fishermen won't believe a straight, slow, up-and-down motion will attract crappies. But actually, this tactic will make crappies bite better during hot months than any other action you can give the lure."

Ingram finds that one of the main advantages to fishing the jigging spoon for summer crappies is that the jigging spoon's weight allows you to fish vertically on top of the cover where you've found the crappies. The ¾-ounce spoon will penetrate almost any cover. You can work the spoon through tree limbs and bushes that you might not normally get through with other crappie lures. For instance, if crappies are holding out near the top of a tree blown down in the water, the only way those fish will see the bait is when it penetrates through the treetop and drops to the trunk's bottom side.

Most anglers fear catching crappies in thick cover because they think they won't be able to get the fish out of the cover. However, this doesn't happen with Ingram's spooning-for-crappies technique.

"I've never had a problem bringing a crappie or a bass up through a treetop on a jigging spoon," he says. "I take my time

Here's proof that the jigging-spoon technique will take both crappies and bass during the summer. Ingram says you'll often find bass and crappies in the same locations.

Jigging Spoons For Crappies

and let the fish wear itself down. Then the crappie generally will come right through all the cover."

Another advantage to fishing the jigging spoon in thick cover during hot weather, according to Ingram, is that you can also take big bass. "When you're fishing the jigging spoon in heavy cover along creek and river channels," he says, "you'll probably catch everything that swims. I've taken saltwater stripers, hybrid striped bass, white bass, bluegills, carp and many catfish. The jigging spoon culls nothing but small fish."

Ingram also does not have to change tackle to switch from bass fishing to crappie fishing.

"I use 17-pound-test Stren line and a baitcasting rod and reel all the time," Ingram says. "I prefer the heavier line for several reasons. Because I expect to catch big fish, 17-pound-test line is usually what's already spooled on my reel. Most crappies I take will weigh from ¾ to 2½ pounds each, and the bass I catch usually will weigh 4 pounds or more. If I get on a big catfish, a stripe or a hybrid, I won't have a prayer of landing the fish if I'm not using at least 17-pound-test line. The heavier line also can take more abuse than lighter line. My line is always rubbing against cover and structure and being nicked and scraped, all of which would weaken lighter line and cause it to break if a good-sized fish strikes."

During summer months, crappies usually will hold in very tight schools. To catch many, an angler may have to fish 15 or 20 different, deep-water sites throughout the lake during a day's time on the lake.

"I often run to 20 spots a day to take a limit of crappies," Ingram says. "What I like about this jigging spoon technique for crappie fishing is you know instantly whether or not you'll catch any fish in an area.

"When I locate stumps, brush or downed trees on the edges of creek or river channels, I know the crappies aren't there if I let the jigging spoon down to the bottom, work it back to the top three times and don't catch a fish. Then I quickly pull up my trolling motor and run to another spot. I don't have to waste time fishing where there are no crappies. Generally, if the crappies are holding on a particular piece of cover, by the time my jigging spoon reaches the bottom the first time, I'll have on a fish. I've caught and released as many as 50 crappies just as fast as I've let my spoon down and brought it back up to the surface on one spot."

Ingram says, "This technique works all year long. Some crappies always are holding on deep-water structure throughout the year, even during the spring. Although crappies do move near the banks to spawn, all the fish don't move to the bank or come off the bank at the same time.

"Another advantage I've found in using this tactic is that just like bass, deep-water crappies are less affected by weather changes than the shallow-water fish," he says. "If rain or a flash flood moves onto a lake, most of the time that stained water won't get deep enough to affect my deep-water crappie fishing. If a radical weather change occurs, the crappies still will be in that deeper water. In the hot weather, when I'm guiding clients to bass, I can take anglers to some of my summertime crappie hotspots and help them catch a box full of fish to take home for a fish fry when the bass aren't biting."

Ingram believes there is an environmental advantage to fishing summertime crappies, as well. "Not only can you continue to catch crappies throughout a summer's day with the jigging spoon," he says, "but you can take your catch home and eat it without fear of detrimentally impacting the resource."

Although for years the jigging spoon has been considered a bass lure, Charlie Ingram has proven it's also one of the most deadly crappie baits. Ingram's jigging-spoon tactic allows not only dedicated crappie fishermen to catch fish during a traditionally difficult time of year, but also bass anglers to catch crappies when bass aren't active.

6

Ultimate Ultra-Light Tackle

by Dave Hrbacek

Steve Pennaz wasn't sure which of two, well-worn proverbs inspired him to revolutionize his approach to ice fishing. Perhaps it was "Necessity is the mother of invention," or maybe "When in Rome, do as the Romans do?" Actually, it may have been both. A few years ago Pennaz, editor of *North American Fisherman*, was in Finland as a member of the U.S. team for the world ice fishing championship, featuring the best hard-water anglers from eight countries, including the now-defunct Soviet Union.

Upon his arrival in Finland, Pennaz had every reason to believe his methods and tackle would work, and he used them during several days of pre-competition fishing. Sure, he caught his share of fish and so did his teammates, but it seemed the European competitors were catching more. That prompted him to quiz them about their fishing system. As it turned out, their tackle was minuscule compared to the tackle Pennaz and his fishing mates were using. Pennaz was using standard American ultra-light tackle: 2- and 4-pound-test line and ice flies with No. 10 hooks. The Europeans were using much smaller tackle: No. 18 (and smaller) hooks, pinhead-sized split shot and line as light as ½-pound test, as well as rods no longer than Pennaz' hand.

Even though he was shocked to see such tiny setups, Pennaz decided to try them. The "ultimate, ultra-light" tackle paid off to the tune of a bronze medal for the American team. All five of the American team members used the system to catch fish. Pennaz

This is all you need to maximize your use of the ultimate ultra-light system for winter bluegills. A fish locator saves an angler time and effort, putting him on a productive location quickly.

Ultimate Ultra-Light Tackle   63

(using a No. 18 hook on a jigging spoon called a pilke, ¾-pound test line, pinhead-sized split shot and a 9-inch European rod) caught one fish during the 4-hour competition—a whitefish weighing 46 grams. His fish brought the U.S. team's total to 622 grams, which tied the Soviet anglers' catch in overall weight. The Americans lost, however, on a tie-breaker. Finland was first with 1,053 grams (2.3 pounds).

Pennaz couldn't believe it—his team had actually outfished some of the European teams using their own methods. Needless to say, he couldn't wait to get home and try the ultimate ultra-light system on his own waters.

"We weren't fishing for small fish," he says, "but when that's the only thing that would hit, then we had to target those fish. We weren't fishing for 1-pound perch, we were fishing for 5-, 6-pound pike. They weren't hitting. So what we did was scale down to find anything that would hit. And by the time we got down to ½-pound test and No. 18 to 22 hooks, the fish that we were then targeting were 4, 5 and 6 inches long, on down to about 2 or 3 inches."

In other words, they were after the same fish as the Europeans were. The most successful angler in the competition caught 38 fish called mutea, which weighed a total of 640 grams (1.4 pounds).

During the 16-hour plane ride home, Pennaz and his teammates contemplated the methods they had learned in Finland. Pennaz wondered if such light tackle could be used at home. It would be a while before he could find out. When he got back, Minnesota's lakes were free of ice. All he could do was vow to break out the ultimate ultra-light tackle during the next ice-fishing season.

"As soon as the ice formed," Pennaz says, "I got out on Lake Minnetonka." (The lake is located in the western suburbs of Minneapolis.) "It was a cold afternoon and I ran into a couple of friends who had been on a known bluegill spot for about two hours. They had two fish between them. I turned on my depthfinder and saw that there were fish down there. In fact, there were a lot of fish down there."

At first, Pennaz tried his regular tackle: 2- to 4-pound test line and an ice fly with a No. 12 hook. He attached a maggot to the ice fly. Despite watching fish on the depthfinder come up to

The tiny rod and the ultimate ultra-light tackle were deadly on this day as indicated by the number of bluegills "on ice." When heavier tackle fails you, switch to the ultimate ultra-light.

his bait, he couldn't entice any of them to hit, even though they followed the bait as he raised it higher and higher.

"I could see them come up to that jig," he says. "They would suck on it. And when they flared their gills, that jig would turn and they'd get about half the maggot in their mouth. So what was happening most of the time is guys would set the hook and miss it because the bluegill didn't have the hook in his mouth."

Pennaz now knew the conventional ultra-light tackle was too heavy. So he switched to the European tackle he had with him. He tied on a No. 18 hook and attached a tiny weight. Within minutes, fish after fish came flopping through the hole. The ultimate ultra-light method was working.

"They would suck it in on the first gulp, and I would catch the fish," Pennaz says. "I was surprised that those hooks stuck. I would lose some fish, but I was catching more than I was missing. I ended up catching and releasing more than 100 fish by the end of the afternoon. There must have been 20 or 30 other guys in the group. I think they had five or six fish between them. A few weeks later, a friend and I did the same thing. Nobody else was catching fish, but we were just hammering 'em."

Ultimate Ultra-Light Tackle

That was all the evidence Pennaz needed. He has been using the system ever since. It is not the only method he uses, but it's one he doesn't hesitate to go to when all else fails. "It's not a cure-all," he says. "But, on those days when you're missing a lot of fish, this is something you should consider."

Tailor Made For Bluegills
The ultimate ultra-light system seems to work best for one type of panfish: bluegills. Pennaz was hoping to use it for crappies and perch, as well, but he soon learned it wasn't the answer for those species.

"I'm targeting bluegills," he says. "I've tried it on crappies, and it doesn't work. The hooks aren't big enough to hold; there are other methods that are better."

Crappies' mouths are too paper-thin and too big for the tiny hooks to be effective. Perch mouths also are too big. Bluegills are another story, Pennaz says. For one thing, their mouths are small enough to warrant the use of tiny hooks. And they have firm flesh throughout the inside of the mouth, making it a perfect sticking ground for small hooks. However, Pennaz has found one other fish species that can be caught with the ultimate ultra-light system, but more on that later.

Small Hooks Net Big Results
The hooks may be one of the smallest parts of the system, but they are the most important. In fact, if anglers do nothing more than change to smaller sized hooks, they'll have a lot to gain.

To adopt the proper frame of mind on hook size, think about trout fishing. Trout enthusiasts think nothing of going to hooks as small as No. 22 for wary trout in clear streams. Ice anglers chasing bluegills should develop the same mentality. The only drawback to using extremely small hooks is that they aren't as easy to find.

"I had trouble finding hooks smaller than No. 12," Pennaz says. "At your typical bait shop, if you buy ice flies, you may find No. 14 and maybe 16, but you'll never find an 18 or a 20 or a 22 because they're just not made."

That is, they're not made in mass quantities and distributed to all-purpose sporting goods stores and bait shops. So those seeking the little hooks should be prepared to go to specialty shops. A simple rule of thumb is this: If a store sells a complete line of fly-

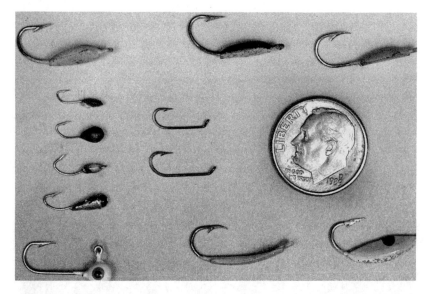

Framed top and bottom by the "standard" ice fishing lures, the hooks used in the ultimate ultra-light system seem pretty small. In the center are Nos. 14 (below) and 16 hooks. Hook sizes at left range from No. 16 to No. 22. (The dime provides a good indication of how small these hooks are.)

fishing supplies, chances are it will carry the smaller hooks.

"I've had good luck with Mustad fly hooks in No. 14 and 16," Pennaz says, "I prefer the 16 because it has thinner wire and I've learned a way to actually thread the maggot completely onto the hook so you can hardly even see the hook. It seems to be incredibly effective."

For those who want to experiment, try Nos. 18, 20 and 22. However, for beginners, Pennaz recommends the 14s and 16s. They'll seem plenty small compared with what most people are using now.

Once you've got the hooks, it's time to doctor them a bit. Pennaz likes to slightly bend the hook gap out to increase hooking percentage. Then, he bends the barb down. "I like to thread the maggot completely on the hook," he says, "not just hook a little tip of it. The pushed-down barb and the light-wire hooks make that easier to do."

Maggots: Best Dressing On Small Hooks

These small-sized hooks leave few options for bait. Minnows are certainly out. That leaves the other two popular winter baits:

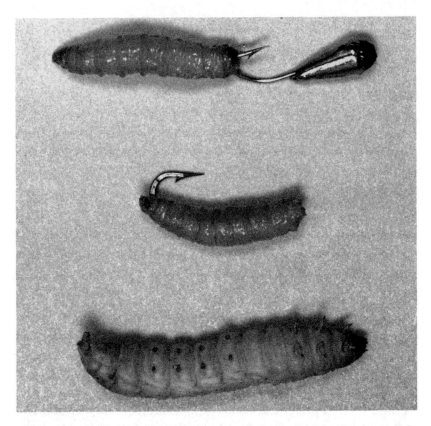

Here are Pennaz' ways of putting the bait on these tiny hooks. A full-sized waxworm at the bottom gives a very good indication of the size of the bait and hook.

waxworms and Eurolarvae (also called maggots). Pennaz uses both, whether fishing European or conventional methods. Each bait has its pros and cons.

His favorite bait (the one he usually starts with) is Eurolarvae. He likes the fact that they come in various colors. They also seem to be tougher than waxworms. And they're more lively on the hook. Maggots will wiggle enticingly on a hook for 20 minutes or more, in much the same manner as a leech.

Despite the maggots' advantages, Pennaz still likes to have a few waxworms on hand. For some unexplainable reason, there are times when waxworms outproduce Eurolarvae by as much as 20-to-1. The main benefit is that the larger waxworms conceal more of the hook. He will thread waxworms on a hook in the same way he threads Eurolarvae.

Complete Angler's Library

In using Eurolarvae, keep in mind an important Pennaz tip on the proper way to hook them: Don't poke your hook through the middle of the maggot. That will cause it to burst. Instead, hook it in the tougher tissue right behind the two black dots on the flat end. The maggot will stay hooked longer, and bluegills are less apt to tear it off. And the maggot won't burst if you don't poke your hook all the way through it. Push it just barely beneath the skin and pull it back through, in the same way you would hook a minnow under the dorsal fin.

Drawing The Fine Line

Choice of the right line is where the system gets interesting. Again, it's time to rethink the traditional concept of ultra-light tackle. That's what Pennaz had to do when he fished in Finland. And afterward, he realized he had adopted the European mentality. "After fishing in Europe, 4-pound test looked like rope to me," he says.

Actually, anything lighter than 2-pound test works fine for this system. While some may have trouble believing that line lighter than 2-pound test even exists, some U.S. line manufacturers are starting to make lighter line. (Berkley now makes 1-pound-test, coldwater line.) One company that specializes in both light line and light tackle is Class Tackle in Louisiana. Obviously, the place to look for this line is in fly-fishing specialty shops. Don't forget, fly fishing tippets are often lighter than 2-pound test.

So when it comes to line, how light is light?

"I've gone down to as light as ½-pound test," Pennaz explains. "But you don't really need to. I like the 1.7-pound test from Class. If you go down too much lighter, you're going to lose fish. Also, lighter line is hard to see on the ice."

In making the transition to lighter line, Pennaz advises anglers to keep in mind why the light line is important. It has nothing to do with spooking fish, so anglers should not base their choice of line weight on water clarity. Rather, line weight affects how easily the bait can be sucked into a fish's mouth.

"The lighter line has less resistance in the water," he says, "so that when a bluegill comes up and sucks the bait, the line is not going to prevent it from pulling it deep into its mouth. A lot of bluegills caught on ice flies are hooked in the lips, whereas a lot of the fish hooked on the plain (No. 14 and smaller) hooks are hooked deeper in their mouths."

(Because fish are hooked deeper with smaller hooks and lighter line, anglers should have some type of hook-removing device. Pennaz recommends using hemostat pliers, which are normally used by surgeons to clamp blood vessels. Such pliers are normally carried in most sporting goods stores.)

Getting The Bait To The Fish

Weights used to pull the bait down to the fish are the smallest part of the ultimate ultra-light system. Weights about the size of shot used in shotgun shells, like No. 6s or 8s, are average for European anglers. The smallest, functional shot is the size of a pinhead, although Pennaz rarely uses split shot this small.

Of course, using smaller split shot in this system makes sense. Light line, small hooks and small bait require less weight to carry them down. And most folks understand the logic of using as little weight as possible to get the bait down to the fish zone. What isn't so obvious about why smaller shot are important is the lesson learned from Pennaz's bluegill-watching session on Lake Minnetonka.

"A lot of the split shot used now are fairly large," he says. "And, a number of times, I've had bluegills and other fish come up and take the split shot, not the jig. So a lot of times, people that have bites think they're missing fish that are hitting their jigs. Actually, they are hitting the split shot. So I've gone to the European shot—the tiny, tiny stuff—when I'm fishing this system. You can spread them out, get the weight down there and you're not attracting fish with larger shot."

That's the key. A chain of small shot is better than one large one. Pennaz will pinch on about four or five shot. The first one will be placed about 6 inches from the hook. Then the rest of them will be attached about 1/16 inch apart. The chain of shot will be about 1 inch long. The only drawback to the small shot is it's not reusable. Anglers should buy large quantities to maintain an adequate supply. Again, the place to look for the shot is a specialty store. Another good place to find small tackle, including split shot, is in mail-order catalogs.

Detecting The Light Bites

Detecting strikes has been made easier with today's high-tech

Steve Pennaz shows the ultimate ultra-light gear in use, and the scrappy bluegill he caught. Note the spring bobber on the mini-rod. The split shot are mere specks on the slivery-thin line.

floats and spring bobbers. So which type is best for this system?

"I like to stick with a spring bobber," Pennaz says, "because it's simpler to use than a slip float. It can get cold in Minnesota and I've had slip floats freeze on my line, making it difficult to adjust for fish that appear at depths above or below the depth I'm fishing."

Yet, the slip float is better for deep-water fishing with longer rods. Pennaz favors slip floats when he is using longer, conventional ice fishing rods. Pennaz finds that the spring bobbers don't work as well on longer rods because they're farther away and, thus, more difficult to see. Pennaz likes to hold a spring bobber close to his face so he can detect even the subtlest movement. The longer the rod, the more difficult it is to see the bobber.

Another advantage of a slip float is that it allows Pennaz to put his bait back down at the same depth he was fishing. This is critical when fishing in deep water (below 10 feet). Once he's onto fish, he doesn't like to waste time getting his bait right to them. Also, a slip float enables him to wind the line onto a reel.

However, bluegills can change depths in an instant. Pennaz likes to be able to adjust as quickly as possible—before the school of fish has moved through. If the fish start changing depths, he likes to go back to a spring bobber. He can move his bait up or down faster. As he's doing that, he'll check his depthfinder to make sure the bait is in the right place. In this way, he can keep his bait in the fish zone as much as possible.

Fish Softly With A Small (Ice-Fishing) Stick

The current American trend in ice-fishing rods is scaled-down versions of summer outfits. Many come equipped with three or more guides and can be used with ultra-light spinning reels. The rods that Pennaz and the European competitors used in the world championships are crude in comparison.

"One of the most effective rods I used in Finland was about a 9-inch piece of stiff wire on a piece of balsa wood with a couple pegs for winding line around it," Pennaz says. "The thing weighed half an ounce. Any bites felt like a whale. That's the ultimate in finesse fishing. If someone wants to get heavily involved in finesse fishing, I would definitely recommend building a short rod (7 to 8 inches) with a small reel for holding line."

When Pennaz fishes for bluegills, he likes to have both longer, American-made rods and the short, European models. For shallow water (10 feet or less), he likes the short rods. They make it easy for him both to watch the spring bobber and look down into the hole to observe bluegill feeding activity. In deeper water, he'll switch to a longer rod with a spinning reel and a slip float, so he can reel line in quickly with the slip-float system.

The only problem with short rods is availability. As far as Pennaz knows, they're not sold anywhere in the U.S. On the other hand, they're not hard to build. At the moment, Pennaz has several rods that he brought back from Europe. And he considers them to be as precious as any $100 graphite rod he owns.

Putting It All Together

So you've finally got the ultimate ultra-light system assembled—small hooks baited with Eurolarvae, a chain of split shot, 1.7-pound test line and a spring bobber on a 9-inch, homemade rod. What comes next? That's up to you. There are no real tricks in using the system—just practice, practice, practice. Actually, just getting the bait down to the bluegills and letting it dance in front of them is about all it takes. When you detect a strike, apply firm, steady pressure and keep the tension on until the fish comes up the hole. Because of the light line, no jerking motion of any kind is recommended.

Another key point about the system is that the often-used fishing cliche, "big bait, big fish; small bait, small fish," does not apply to the European ice-fishing system. One of his many bluegill forays on a lake close to home disproved this theory.

"I fished this system late in the year and hooked an enormous number of bass—big, big fish," he says. "It was fun while it lasted, but I never got any of them in the hole. The little hooks just didn't hold."

It may take a little time on the ice, but there's no reason why someone using this system can't fill a bucket with bluegills the first time. Pennaz, in fact, has introduced numerous fishing friends to the system with excellent results. Like all other types of fishing, confidence is the key.

7

Summer Perch
With John Lucas

======= by Mike Bleech =======

When asked how he got started fishing for yellow perch, John Lucas explains, "We'd go down to Lake Erie, near Cleveland, Gordon Park, Bay Village. There were long rock piers going out into the lake. You could catch perch there all through the summer, but the best time was April through mid-June. We caught a lot of perch …"

John pauses on the word *perch,* and there is a distant look in his eyes as his mind drifts back. Then he continues, "It was great. I'd say I grew up on perch. We'd ride 15 miles on our bikes to go perch fishing."

John Lucas lives in Warren, Pennsylvania, but he grew up in the Cleveland, Ohio-area, near the rich water of Lake Erie. He has fished for yellow perch and other species throughout the Midwest, the East and eastern Canada. His most notable angling accomplishment was being crowned "King of Pennsylvania Anglers," a reward for winning the 1989 Pennsylvania State Championship Fishing Tournament.

Simple fishing methods that John learned as a boy along Lake Erie are the foundation of his current expertise, which he shares freely. "The best strategy I knew back then was my spot on the breakwall," he says. "You had to get to your spot to secure it. That's breakwall strategy."

The phrase, "Perch are not everywhere or just anywhere," never really sinks home with most anglers. But to an inquisitive,

John Lucas finds that perch love small jigs tipped with bait. He has refined his tactics, however. He now strives to catch large perch instead of numbers of perch.

observant angler, it opens up a never-ending series of questions.

In the early 1960s, John used fishing tackle that was typical of that period—solid fiberglass rods, spincast reels spooled with stiff monofilament line, two snelled hooks on a spreader rig, and a half-ounce or more of lead at the line's end. He used emerald shiners that he had caught with a dip net alongside the breakwall for bait. John cast his baits into weedbed openings, and fed out line so the bait dropped straight down. If it swung back toward him on a tight line it would often swing into weeds. Waves would drag the baits into weeds.

"Those spreader rigs really snagged in the weeds, but we liked them," he says. "Because when the perch were hitting good, we'd catch them two at a time."

John's perch-fishing methods have changed a lot since he was a boy. Some changes have been for greater efficiency. Some have been for the sport. Perch fishing is one of the more rewarding kinds of fishing. Success is normal; yet, it comes at different levels, and in different ways. John's goals are having a good time, and trying to catch the biggest perch available wherever he is fishing.

Quantity doesn't matter; John believes moderation is the proper attitude to have when fishing. Besides, he said, "Filleting perch half of the night is not my idea of fun."

Making Perch Fishing Sporty

Ultra-light tackle is John's choice, whenever practical. Perch are good fighters when they are not overmatched by tackle. You won't break into a sweat while fighting one, but you probably will break into a broad grin.

The rod is the most critical piece of gear in perch fishing. It should be sensitive enough to detect the sometimes light strikes of perch. Equally important, it should be lightweight, so it will flex under the run of frisky perch.

"I want to feel everything the perch does," John says. "I want to feel the perch when he sucks in the jig. I want to feel every wiggle when that perch tries to scoot off into the weeds."

John's favorite perch-fishing outfit is a 5½-foot-long rod, and an ultra-light spinning reel spooled with premium, 4-pound-test monofilament line. The line is a fine-diameter type, clear or colored for low visibility. "Perch aren't line shy," John explains. "I use light line for the sport."

Using small jigs and ultra-light tackle makes perch fishing a lot more exciting for Lucas. The lightweight gear emphasizes the perch's scrappy nature.

Another reason for selecting low-visibility line is that he, like most anglers, uses the same ultra-light outfit for other fish, some of which *are* line shy. A couple line-shy fish that he frequently encounters while perch fishing are bluegills and crappies.

"In most of the waters I have fished," he says, "I've found other panfish. While you're looking for perch, try not to get sidetracked on the large bluegills or crappies. Sometimes I get sidetracked ... I get sidetracked a lot.

"You go fishing for something else, but you run into these nice perch," he continues, "and you fish for them. It's just taking advantage of something."

John's favorite terminal rig is a jig tipped with a small piece of bait. This rig is simple to rerig after losing one to snags, inexpensive and it casts well. It looks, smells and tastes lifelike. And most

Tipping Jigs With Small Bait Pieces

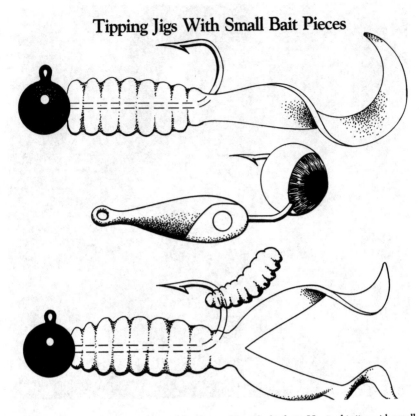

John Lucas likes to add an inducement for the perch to take his bait. He tips his jigs with small pieces of bait, as shown here, so perch can easily get the bait and the hook into their mouths.

important, perch like it. In fact, they like it a lot.

Because they are so versatile, leadheads and soft plastic bodies make up the bulk of his perch tackle. By dressing leadheads with plastic bodies, he can quickly change colors, sizes and shapes. Three or four sizes of leadheads, from 1/32 ounce to 1/4 ounce will handle most depths. The size and shape of the plastic bodies will also affect the sinking rate. This is a handy thing to know when he needs weight for casting distance, or for casting into the wind when he does not want the jig to sink too fast. A 1/16-ounce leadhead dressed with a bulky body will sink at about the same rate as a 1/32-ounce leadhead dressed with a small body; however, the heavier jig will cast better.

Teardrop jigs and jigging spoons are also part of John's perch fishing arsenal. Vertical jigging with spoons is effective in deep water, as long as the boat is still or drifting slowly. Teardrop jigs, more popular among ice anglers than summertime anglers, work well under floats.

Perch are not fussy eaters. They will eat just about any critter that does not eat them. Color and flash are the most important visibility factors, designed to instill confidence in anglers. The little plastic bags filled with jig bodies and leadheads in John's tackle box include chartreuse, white, red, orange, yellow, smoke, clear with metal flakes of various colors and several dot-and-stripe combinations. But if you check the end of John's line occasionally, you will usually see chartreuse or white, unless some other color has been hot for a few days. The addition of a small piece of bait on the jig is more important than the color or shape of the plastic body. The bait's smell will bring the perch, and the taste will bring them back for more if you fail on the first attempt to hook them. Grubs, minnow pieces and perch eyes are John's usual perch baits; however, he is experimenting with freeze-dried grubs and artificial-taste baits.

John doesn't use live minnows. "If the perch are on," he says, "I can take them faster than someone who has to rebait every time. It takes longer for a live minnow to sink to the bottom, and sometimes the minnow hangs in the weeds. I can do more with a jig and a small minnow piece than someone using a whole minnow. That's a razor's edge right there. I don't want the perch monkeying around with the bait. I want them to take it in right now!"

How the lures are used is more important than color or shape. Do not make perch work to catch them; these fish are not the most efficient predators in the lake. Lures should be worked slowly.

Dialing In

The best perch rig in the world "can't catch 'em where they ain't." While John can almost always find perch, he does not try to understate the importance of good location techniques. Still, this does not mean finding perch is difficult. John calls this process of putting tackle, methods and location all together *dialing in*. John advises anglers to stay away from spots that produce only small perch. Most successful anglers fish good waters. You are going to catch your share of good-sized perch if you spend any time at all fishing Lake Erie or the Finger Lakes (of upstate New York). John lives close enough to these lakes for a day of fishing, and close enough to Chautauqua Lake for a half-day excursion. Several lakes, rivers and creeks are within striking distance for John, but he heads for the water where he knows perch fishing is hot.

"Communication provides an edge in perch fishing," John says. "I make a call here, a call there. Sometimes I spend as much time on communication as I do on the entire fishing trip." John will ask anyone who will listen for fishing information. He phones his network of fishing friends, bait shops and boat ramps.

However, information from other anglers simply reveals how they are doing. If you hear that everyone on the lake is doing something that is enough to satisfy you, then do the same thing," John explains. "But, if it isn't enough to satisfy you, then you have to do something different."

Sometimes he'll do something completely different from what anyone else is doing, or go somewhere no one else is fishing. That does not mean he ignores what he hears; it is his nature to do it differently. If anglers on the lake are catching 12-inch perch, he will look for 13-inch fish.

Where does John look? Perch might be just about anywhere. They are probably the most adaptable fish in most lakes. In any given lake, you might find them at the same time in 3 feet of water and in the lake basin's deepest part, on steep structure and over vast flats, in weeds and over bare bottom. Perch are willing to feed in several different ways, wherever they find something to eat.

"If you have a lake basin with just a couple sticks, those sticks become the gathering places," John says. "But if you have a lake that is filled with weeds with just a couple bare spots, then those bare spots become gathering places."

In weedy lakes, John likes to work the edges. Most gamefish inhabiting weedy lakes like to stay on the edges, because the weed edge offers predators cover from which they can attack passing schools of smaller fish. (Sometimes perch are the predators; sometimes they are the prey.) The weed edges are particularly good feeding areas for perch and other panfish because there is also abundant food in the weeds. Many small fish and insects live among the weeds. Edges mean variety.

John likes fishing weedbed edges because they are the ideal environment for his ultra-light tackle and small jigs. He drifts along the longer weedlines when the wind is right, or turns on his electric motor so he can troll slowly while casting the jig ahead of

Working weed patches where perch like to hang out takes a slightly different approach when you're using ultra-light tackle. The illustration on the next page shows why it works.

the boat. Controlling the lure and maintaining sensitivity (difficult skills to master in a moving boat) are keys to a successful operation. The trick is learning how to avoid slack in the line.

Perch usually are in schools of similar-sized individuals. When John catches one that suits him, he will pause as long as he continues to catch perch. Sometimes he can catch all he wants from one place. "I prefer to fish holes in the weedbeds rather than weedlines because perch are more congregated in the holes," he says. "They're more spread out along the weedlines. The best way to fish holes in the weedbed is with a jig-and-bobber rig."

An advantage of the jig-and-bobber rig is that it keeps the line out of the weeds. The line stays above the weeds up to the bobber; then it goes straight down. Another advantage is that the jig stays at the desired depth, determined by the length of the line between the bobber and jig. Lure control is better because the bobber shows what the jig is doing, including the indication of light strikes.

One drawback, however, to the jig-and-bobber rig is hook-setting. Because the line doesn't go straight from the rodtip to the lure, it is more difficult to get enough muscle into the hookset.

Jig-Bobber Rig For Fishing Weeds

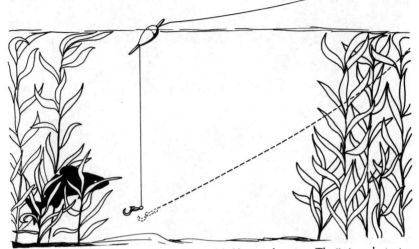

When fishing in weeds, Lucas will use a jig-and-bobber combination. The jig is at the proper depth, and the line doesn't get hung up in the weeds. This is about the only way to fish pockets without spending most of your fishing time clearing your bait.

This is not a big problem with perch because they do not have hard mouths. Another drawback is that this rig is awkward to cast. Two weights—the jig and the bobber—separated by a few feet of line is unwieldy.

"Sometimes I use a slip bobber," John says, "when I want the jig deeper that 5 feet, or so. That's about as much line as I can cast with a 5½-foot rod. But slip bobbers do not work very well with light jigs. It's not enough weight to pull the line through the slip bobber. I think a long rod might be a better way to fish deeper water, to a point. I'd like to have a nice 7- to 7½-foot ultra-light rod. I can fish about a rod length of line below the bobber."

Deeper water presents problems for ultra-light tackle. Ultra-light rods are generally suited for lures that weigh less than a quarter ounce, but heavier weights are necessary to search for perch in water deeper than 15 feet. In this situation, John uses heavier balanced tackle to find the perch; then, if it is practical, he switches to ultra-light tackle once the perch are pinpointed.

"In the summer I catch bigger perch, on average, from deeper water," he says. "Perch might be easier to catch in the weeds, but usually they're smaller. The biggest perch will be scattered along the deep flats, and you just have to find them. Sometimes you have to keep moving. It doesn't pay to stop when you get a perch because the perch are moving. If you stop you would be fishing where they were, not where they are."

Using two baits, or bait-lure combinations, on short leaders with a heavy weight on the end of the line is one way John will search for perch in deep water. This strategy is based upon one of the most popular drift-fishing rigs used in Lake Erie. It is effective, depending upon drift speed, to at least 60 feet with the only limitation being the amount of weight you are willing to use. However, perch can usually be found in less than 60 feet of water.

John's deep-water rig is novel in that he uses weights which are lead-cast to a V-shaped wire. This is instead of the chugging irons (lead weights cast to the middle of a long wire) that have

Deep-Water Drift Fishing Rig

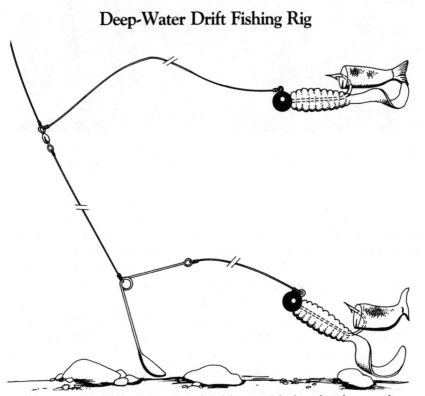

Using a variation of the old deep-water drift-fishing rig, John has adapted a newer bottom-bouncing weight in which the weight is at one end of a V-shaped wire. The lures are soft-plastic jig bodies on fine-wire, long-shank hooks.

Because Lucas fishes for perch year-round, he puts his ultra-light tackle aside when perch are in deep water. Now it's time to use heavier baitcasting gear for drift fishing in deep water.

been popular on Lake Erie for many years. His lures are the same soft plastic bodies he uses on leadheads, except that they are rigged on long shank hooks instead of leadheads. The line should be at least 10-pound test, because the rig will often snag.

A ¾-ouncer will stay close to the bottom in depths of at least 20 feet. A 1½-ounce weight should be enough to pull the lures down to 40 feet. If not, then the drift might be too fast. One or more drift anchors should ensure an appropriate drifting speed. John keeps his rigs close to bottom by touching it with the weight occasionally, and by watching the sonar.

"You don't want it really dragging," he says.

Drifting is not a random process to John, at least not to begin with. "I have to work the breaks first, before working the vast expanse of bare bottom," he says.

John is a dedicated structure fisherman. Even when perch are working the flats, John speculates that the most likely places to catch perch will be on irregular structure. The first places he tries are along a flat's edges, particularly steep edges. Then he will look for structure in the midst of the flat. Constrictions in the flat are often hotspots. These constrictions, usually a point or a pair of points, concentrate moving perch like a bottleneck.

This is where sonar skill comes in handy. John spends a lot of time studying his sonar screen. "I look at that sonar carefully when I catch perch," John says, "to see if there is anything special down there."

Maps are another important part of John's fishing system. Looking for structure without a map is like stumbling around in the dark. Small details which are not shown on the map are penciled in when John finds them.

Most anglers tend to take their perch fishing less seriously than other kinds of fishing. That's fine because perch still can be caught by anglers with that kind of attitude. That is the beauty of these accommodating, tasty fish. John takes all of his fishing seriously. That is what makes him happy. You can put his methods to good use whether you want to get serious about perch or not. Either way, it's a good time.

Catfish

8

Tailrace Catfish

by John Phillips

Bubbling and swirling, the swift waters of tailraces make anglers think of catfish, feeding in the current's boils and foam in the highly oxygenated water. But sometimes those catfish are hard to catch. John Hill of Town Creek, Alabama, has solved the riddle of taking tailrace cats. Hill owns and operates a fishing camp on the banks of the Tennessee River. For more than 20 years, Hill has spent several days a week in the tailrace area watching anglers catch catfish as well as taking catfish himself.

In the late spring and early summer, enough catfish are taken from this Wheeler Dam tailrace to supply area fish markets, and some anglers earn a living catching catfish on hook and line, rather than with commercial catfishing tactics.

However, not all anglers who frequent the Wheeler Dam tailrace consistently catch catfish. This is because they have not learned the secrets of tailrace cats. These secrets not only are deadly effective on the Tennessee River but in most tailraces throughout the nation.

"The key to catching catfish in tailraces is being able to read the water and knowing just where the catfish are," Hill says.

Although catfish roam most tailrace areas below dams because of the abundant baitfish in the water and the highly oxygenated flow coming through the turbines, some parts of a tailrace will produce more catfish than others. (However, productive spots may switch abruptly.)

A hefty stringer of catfish like this one is not just a dream for serious catfishermen, as long as they know how to fish tailraces like John Hill. There is more to it than fishermen realize.

Tailrace Catfish   89

Finding The Current Grooves

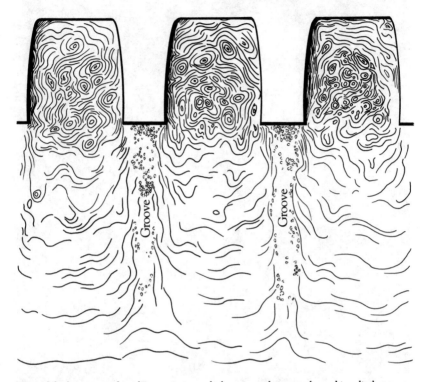

One of the keys to catching big cats is to work the grooves between the turbine discharges, as indicated in this illustration. The grooves are the slowest part of the swift water.

According to Hill, "Noting the amount of water coming through the turbines, learning which turbines are and aren't running, distinguishing changes in the turbines' water flow, and knowing where underwater stocks are located are critical factors for finding tailrace catfish."

Find Converging Current Groves
The fastest flow from a turbine's discharge is in the center. As the discharge diminishes, Hill says, the slowest water is on the flow's outer edge. When two turbines are running side by side or close to each other, the surface water all appears to be moving at the same speed. However, the two currents actually collide with each other so the water is slower where the currents meet. This slow water, between two, fast-moving currents is called a groove.

"Catfish are not dumb," Hill says. "Although they will feed in the swift water, they are looking for the slowest part of the swift water in which to hold and feed. The grooves provide that slack-water area."

Out of a large number of anglers fishing in a tailrace area, anglers in certain boats regularly catch more catfish than those in boats fishing only a few yards away. The successful anglers have learned where the grooves are, how the currents collide and where the fish are holding along the bottom. Learning to read the grooves is like having an invisible road map that leads to the catfish no one else in the tailrace can find. By staying on the groove, you can catch catfish until the current changes and they move.

"The reason the cats move is turbine flow. Turbines at many dams are automatic," Hill says. "These turbines increase and de-

While catfish like this will feed in swift water, they find the slowest part of the current in which to feed. "Catfish aren't dumb," Hill says.

crease the water flow as the power requirements are met. Even though the turbines continue to run, the discharge flow may change two or three times during the day. When the flow varies, the cats often will move and search out more slack water in which to feed." That's why anglers who change locations several times during the day usually catch more catfish in tailrace areas than those who sit in one spot.

"When the cats stop biting in one groove, then you can assume the flow has changed," Hill says. "Move to find another groove full of cats. While converging currents create the grooves, the flow determines which groove is the most productive."

Search For Rock Grooves

Another kind of groove that successful tailrace fishermen learn to find is a rock groove. "Successfully fishing a rock groove requires using a quality depthfinder," Hill says. "Assume that the bottom of the tailrace is not flat, because most tailraces have rocky bottoms. Use the depthfinder to spot the big rocks on the bottom. Once you find the rocks, though, you cannot mark them with buoys because of the swift water. Therefore, it is important to remember the location of these submerged rocks.

"If you are drift fishing, let your boat drift over the rocks while you bump your bait over and behind the rocks. The catfish will be lying directly behind the rocks in the slack water created by the rocks. If the boulder is large enough, this groove of slack water could extend for 30 or 40 yards behind the rock.

"If you prefer to anchor your boat upstream of the rock groove," Hill says, "bump the bottom back to the rock, and let your bait wash around the rock. Then bump the bait back down the groove until you catch a cat. Both tactics work equally well. Another advantage is that the underwater rock grooves aren't visible, so most anglers never figure out how you managed to catch catfish—even if they are fishing right next to you."

Best Rigs For Groove Fishing

Kyle Baggett of Cullman, Alabama, was a tailrace specialist in taking cats for over 30 years. Many of the tactics Hill utilizes were learned from Baggett. Baggett knew catfish and their habits. No matter what the water or weather conditions, or whether the fish were feeding, Baggett brought in 50 to 100 pounds of cats every

Baggett's Bottom Bumping Rig

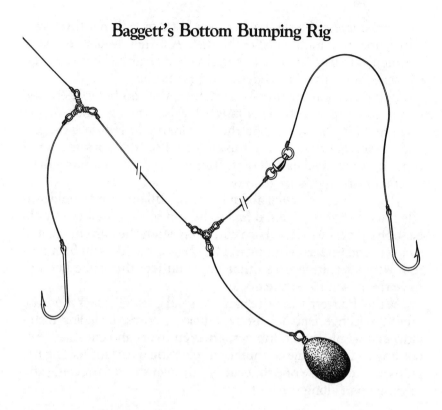

This illustration shows graphically how Kyle Baggett tied his bottom-bumping rig. Note the barrel swivel in the line to the bottom hook. This reduces twist in the line.

day. In addition to advocating groove fishing, Baggett believed that proper rigging was a key to successful tailrace catfishing.

From Baggett, Hill learned how to use a bottom-bumping rig, which consists of a 4- to 5-ounce weight and an 8-inch, 20-pound-test monofilament drop line, both attached to the eyes of a three-way swivel. The weight is attached 12 to 18 inches below the swivel. To the drop line, Baggett would attach either a No. 1 or a No. 2 bait-holder hook. A barrel swivel between the hook and the swivel's eye keeps the bait from twisting the main line as it rolls in the current.

According to Hill, Baggett chose a bait-holder hook because it would hold the gizzard shad gut that he usually used in fishing the tailrace. Baggett would run the hook through the shad's entrails, sliding them up against the hook's eye.

To complete the rig, Baggett would tie on another three-way swivel about 10 inches above the first. A 6-inch leader and hook is attached to this swivel. No barrel swivel is needed here because the three-way swivel provides enough rotation.

Using the shorter line for attaching the top hook keeps the two hooks from becoming entangled. Also, the top hook should ride higher in the water than the bottom hook. Hill says Baggett had found that catfish won't always feed on the bottom; sometimes they will feed just off of it. In that case, more catfish will be caught on the top hook than on the bottom hook.

Baggett was particular about his rods, Hill says, and would usually build his own. The rod had to be stiff so that the hook could be set hard at the first feel of a cat, even when the current created a bow in the line. According to Hill, Baggett used a stiff fiberglass rod with a sensitive tip so that he could feel the strike but still have the power to set the hook.

While Baggett's favorite bait was shad guts, Hill says there are other productive baits for fishing tailrace grooves, including nightcrawlers, whole shad minnows, chicken livers and cut shad. According to Hill, a rule of thumb in selecting a bait for fishing the grooves is to choose one that catfish are accustomed to seeing and feeding upon along the bottom.

Fishing Tailraces With Jugs

One of the easiest, most productive methods of catching cats in a tailrace, in states where it's allowed, is to jug fish for them. (Be sure to check local and state restrictions.)

"Usually, sometime from late spring through October, jug fishing will be productive," Hill says. "Most jug fishermen will put out 25 to 50 jugs in the calm water to the side and below the spillways. If a number of turbines are running and there is no wind, the current will pull the jugs from that calm water over toward the swift water. The current may be very slight, but it still will cause the jugs to move. Cats often will concentrate and feed in that slack water and light current."

Another place that produces numbers of catfish in tailraces below dams with locks is the lock impoundment—where discharge water is released. In high-traffic situations where discharge water is forced out of the impoundment regularly, currents that draw shad are created. With the shad come the catfish.

Jug fishing below a dam can be very effective. The jugs are placed in the calm water on the sides, and the current pulls them toward the swifter water, over the catfish's prime feeding areas.

"When traffic on the river is heavy, jug fishing around this discharge water current can be extremely productive," Hill says. "No matter which side of the blow hole, as we call it at Wheeler, that you put your jugs on, cats will come from all directions into this part of the tailrace. Your catch may average 3 to about 20 pounds each."

Most anglers use pint or quart jugs with 6 feet of line tied to the jug's neck, a piece of shot lead, either a 1/0 or a No. 1 hook and bait with live shad minnows if they can get them. The yellow cat seems to like the live shad minnow better than any bait, and channels and blues also will take the live shad minnow. Hook the minnow from the bottom lip to the top lip to keep it alive and allow it to swim. Shad guts and chicken guts also are used for baiting jugs and will produce catfish.

Tailrace Catfish   95

A cooler full of cats! That's the reward for learning how to fish tailraces effectively. These fish were taken on jugs, an effective way of taking summer catfish. The discharge draws shad, and the shad draw the catfish.

According to Hill, the difference between those who land cats on jugs and those who don't land them often is the finesse used when leading a catfish to the boat. Most jug fishermen use either 30-pound-test monofilament or No. 9 trotline staging. (You'll learn more about jug fishing in chapter 9.)

"However, line that strong makes tearing the hook out of the catfish's mouth or straightening the hook very easy. The best way to land a cat is to pick up the jug and hold it in your hand (palm up). Don't wrestle the cat into the boat. Gently lead the fish to the surface, get your net under it and put the fish in the boat.

"If the catfish sees the boat and starts to run, drop the jug and let the fish take it under. You can try to land the fish again when the jug comes back up. You will land more cats using less pressure than you will if you attempt to horse them into the boat."

9

Of Plastic Jugs And Thermoclined Cats

by Harry Ryan

Sometime during the summer, catfish seem to mysteriously disappear from many of America's ponds and impoundments. Catfish anglers have long recognized this phenomenon, but few know how to catch these bewhiskered bottom-dwellers when the summer slump sets in. "I'd venture to say that virtually every catfish angler in America who floats a boat in farm ponds, small lakes and even in some impoundments, has experienced the summer slump at one time or another," says Chris Altman, an outdoor writer and catfishing authority from Pikeville, Kentucky. Altman is the author of NAFC's Complete Angler's Library book, *Catfishing*.

"The summer slump experienced by catfish anglers is nothing more than an aquatic environment phenomenon that actually prevents cats from roaming the pond's deeper regions," Altman says. This phenomenon is called thermal stratification. It is something that catfish anglers must understand and deal with to be successful when fishing a thermally stratified body of water.

The Stratification Of Summer

"In the hot summer months, a vague water layer called the *thermocline* dictates the lower depth where cats feed and survive in our impoundments," says Altman. Understanding the thermocline and why thermal stratification occurs helps the angler catch more cats during those lean summer months.

"As the water temperature changes, so does its density. Be-

A 25-pound blue catfish is a nice reward for a night's work. Chris Altman took this beauty at a depth of about 4 feet in a thermally stratified lake. Knowing the effects of stratification can pay big dividends.

Of Plastic Jugs And Thermoclined Cats   99

Summer Stratification In Lakes, Ponds

The three layers of a stratified lake or pond are detailed in this illustration. Obviously, the epilimnion or lowest layer is not a hospitable area for catfish, or any other species in summer.

cause cold water is heavier, or more dense, than warm water," Altman explains, "the cold water sinks beneath the warmer water. In this manner, a body of water separates into three layers of decreasing water temperatures during extended periods of hot weather. This occurs in most ponds and small lakes, and even in some larger impoundments that lack a regular, distinct and relatively strong current."

The top layer, or epilimnion, is circulated by the wind and wave action and remains well-oxygenated throughout the summer. In lakes that stratify, most aquatic life is found in this upper layer.

The middle layer, or thermocline, is a relatively narrow band of water characterized by a rapid decrease (technically speaking, .548 degrees Fahrenheit per foot) in temperature. "In larger impoundments, the thermocline often develops 15 to 25 feet below the surface," Altman says. "In smaller ponds, however, the thermocline may actually be found just 5 or 6 feet deep. As a rule of thumb, the bottom of the thermocline layer dictates the deepest point at which you can find catfish, so it is a vital piece of knowledge for the angler."

In all stratified bodies of water, the layer of cold water below the thermocline, called the *hypolimnion*, has so little dissolved oxygen that it becomes uninhabitable. "The levels of dissolved oxygen in this layer also decrease as the season progresses," Altman says. "You may find catfish in the hypolimnion shortly after the pond stratifies. As a rule, though, they tend to vacate it rather quickly."

Catfish are, for the most part, a deep-water, bottom-dwelling species, so anglers are accustomed to looking for them in deeper holes on the lake bottom. "But," says Altman, "when the lake stratifies, the cats leave the deeper areas because conditions (primarily dissolved oxygen levels) are more favorable for them in shallower water. Now catfish anglers have to do a little detective work to find the cats."

Locating The Thermocline

Through the years, Altman has learned several ways to pinpoint the thermocline's location. "The easiest and most convenient method is simply using your depthfinder," he says. "By cranking up the sensitivity on your liquid-crystal unit or paper graph, you can usually see the thermocline on the screen. Most often, the sensitivity has to be increased to the halfway point or higher before the thermocline becomes visible. On a liquid-crystal unit, it appears as a horizontal line across the screen. On a paper graph, it appears as a gray, hazy, poorly defined band across the paper." What the sonar unit is picking up, says Altman, is a "mud" layer that forms in the thermocline, rather than the actual thermocline itself. This "mud" consists of dead algae and plankton that has sunk to a depth at which the material becomes neutrally buoyant and then suspends. Most often, this occurs within the thermocline.

Another means of locating the 'cline is by using a portable temperature probe or one of the combination (temperature/color/pH) units now marketed. "These units usually have a probe suspended on a coaxial cable which is marked in 1-foot increments.

By lowering the probe 1 foot at a time, you can actually map the thermocline by simply watching the temperature change on the unit's meter. When the probe reaches the thermocline, the temperature drops rapidly, about half a degree per foot of depth," Altman explains. "When the probe exits the bottom of the thermocline, the temperature continues to fall, but at a much slower rate."

Some successful anglers have learned to simply suspend their baits at about the lake's mid-depth point during the late-summer months. If they fail to get a bite at that depth, they'll begin raising their bait about 1 or 2 feet at a time until they find the cats," Altman says.

Capitalizing On The 'Cline

After pondering the effects of thermal stratification on catfish, an angler might conclude that the best strategy is to target those lake bottoms that are above the thermocline. While that approach certainly puts cats in your livewell, Altman has learned that a high percentage of catfish do not hold or relate to any type of physical structure.

"Cats often relate to the thermocline as they would to a physical structure," Altman says. "In other words, a lot of the cats suspend on top of the thermocline, lying on the water seam just as if it were the lake's bottom. The problem is that they may be anywhere in the lake, just suspending out in open water, and this makes them rather difficult to locate."

At this time, catfish suspend in the lake's middle, as well as along the shoreline, so an angler's best bet is to use a technique that covers a great deal of water. Altman's weapon of choice is the catfishing jug, a rather primitive tool by most standards, but nevertheless a tremendously productive one. By attaching a baited hook and line to a floating jug and then releasing the rig to float away, a vast amount of water can be covered even during the angler's absence. "Jug fishing is, without question, the most effective technique to catch catfish in a thermally stratified body of water," he says.

The Fall Turnover

When the air temperature drops in early autumn, cool night temperatures cause the lake's layers to begin mixing. This renews

Fall Turnover

The fall turnover brings oxygen into all depths of the lake so that catfish will return to the depths again. They're also hungry feeders during this period, but more difficult to find.

the oxygen levels and distributes nutrients throughout the lake, effectively ending jug fishing. Autumn storms and heavy winds help speed the process which, in time, rejuvenates the lake from top to bottom. This is known as the fall turnover. Shortly after this occurs, catfish can again be found at any depth. Often, a lake turns a dark brown color and emits a sulfurous "swamp gas" odor.

"When the turnover occurs, jugging basically goes to pot," Altman says. "The catfish typically move to deeper areas where they are beyond a jug line's reach, and they most likely haunt the lake's deeper holes throughout the winter months.

Gearing Up

Although catfishing jugs can be made from virtually any plastic container that has a screw-on lid, Altman prefers to use 1-

How To Make A Catfish Jug

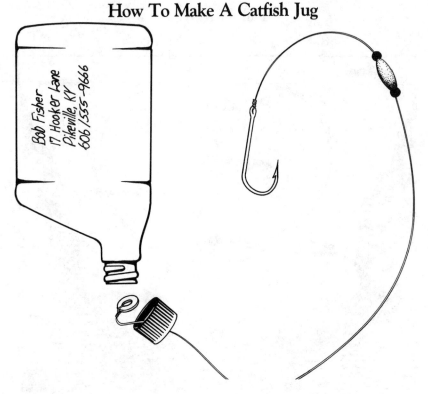

Altman's design for effective jug fishing is simple and to the point. Drill a small hole in the screw cap of a 1-quart plastic oil container, tie your line to a washer and run the line out the hole in the cap. Then add the tackle and you're set.

quart, plastic, motor-oil bottles. "The problem with larger bottles such as milk jugs is that they take up too much room in the boat," he says. Put 40 or 50, gallon-sized jugs in your boat and they'll blow out of the boat at the most inopportune times."

Oil jugs, on the other hand, are compact and easy to stash in the livewells and your boat's dry-storage compartments. Although they are small, these 1-quart jugs will tire even a 25- to 30-pound catfish.

To make his catfishing jugs, Altman drills a small hole through the screw-on lid and runs a piece of nylon cord through the hole. Next, he ties a metal washer to the line that extends from the inside of the lid. Finally, he simply drops the washer into the bottle, screws on the lid and ties a hook and sinker onto the line's terminal end extending from the bottle.

"Another thing I like about using oil jugs with screw-on lids is that it's easy to change the line's length," Altman says. "To shorten the line, simply push the excess into the jug, slip a loop around the threaded spout and screw the cap back on. That might not seem too secure, but the cats cannot put too much pressure on it because the floating jug gives the catfish nothing to pull against."

While he uses clean, 1-quart oil jugs for most of his jug fishing, Altman also uses larger jugs on occasion. "In larger lakes and impoundments, I often use larger jugs that can be seen at greater distances. Two-liter pop bottles work well, and most of them have a lip molded around the neck that allows you to tie your line around the bottle's neck. Because they are made of clear plastic, you should paint the bottles bright colors to increase their visibility,"

While Altman prefers to make his own jugs for catching cats, others prefer to buy ready-made jugs. They tend to be smaller for easier storage, and brightly colored for easy viewing.

Of Plastic Jugs And Thermoclined Cats

he says. "It may sound strange, but I've found that white jugs are the most visible across a large expanse of water. Yellow or fluorescent orange are easily spotted, too.

"I put average-sized baits on my oil-jug rigs, but I also carry a few 2-liter pop bottles or gallon-sized milk jugs to use with big baits when I want to catch a big cat," Altman explains. One problem that Altman has found in using a smaller jug is that a large cat can pull it underwater far enough to snag the line on structure of some sort. If this happens, you may never find the jug or the cat you hooked."

Whatever jug type you use, be sure to carry several with you. "Fifteen to 20 jugs per angler makes for an entertaining evening," Altman says. "Any more than that and the play turns into work." However, be sure to check local regulations on the legality of jug fishing. Some states have a limit on the number of jugs allowed per angler, and many require anglers to mark each jug with a name, address and phone number.

Altman suggests recording, on the top of each jug, the line length used. By doing this, you can quickly determine the depth at which most cats are feeding and then adjust the depth on your other jugs accordingly. "If you find that you are catching most of your fish at a depth of 6 or 8 feet," he says, "then you should immediately adjust all of your lines to that length. In ponds and small lakes with relatively shallow thermocline, 5 to 10 feet of line is usually all you need. In larger lakes where the thermocline may form 15 to 25 feet below the surface, you need to use longer line."

Rigging the jugs is simple. A ¼- to 1-ounce sinker is tied to the line about 18 to 24 inches above the hook. Using live baits on longer lines requires heavier sinkers than when using cut bait on shorter lines. Generally, a 1/0 or 2/0 hook is sufficient for most jug-fishing chores, although Altman sometimes uses hooks as large as a 5/0 when baiting the jug rig with a hand-sized bluegill or an 8-inch creek chub.

"I've baited my jugs with virtually everything imaginable through the years," he says. "On occasion, almost anything will catch catfish. My favorite bait for use on a smaller jug is a 4- or 5-inch creek minnow that is trapped before going to the lake. To catch big cats, I use big bluegills. The struggles of a live fish tend to attract cats. Cut bait made from shad, bluegill or even carp is usually fairly productive, although not on par with a live offer-

This channel cat tipped the scales at over 13 pounds. Catfish feed more actively at night so it is a good time to get the jugs out and have some fun catching big cats.

ing." As a general rule, Altman doesn't use soft baits like chicken liver and stink baits for jug fishing because little cats pick the hooks clean before a big cat ever finds the bait. And big cats can steal a soft bait without hooking themselves.

More Jug Fishing Basics

Jug fishing is most often done at night. One reason is that catfish feed most actively during the night. Also, floating jugs pose a very real hazard for water skiers and boating traffic, both of which are mainly daylight activities. A third reason is that if the lake has gar, those snaggy-toothed fish often pick your baited hooks clean during the day.

Some anglers drop their jugs, planning to check on them periodically throughout the night. This can become angling's ver-

Altman recommends putting jugs out in front of a creek arm or in "contained" areas (as being done here) of lakes, then let the wind or wave action (if any) help keep them contained. Also try different depths.

sion of hide-and-seek or cat-and-mouse games, providing a full night's entertainment for those anglers with tendencies toward insomnia. Others drop their jugs around sundown and check on them early the next morning. Of course, the number of fish you can take this way is limited to the number of jugs you put out.

Wind direction obviously plays a vital role in jug fishing. If you drop the baited rigs upwind, the jugs are carried across the water. By selecting the lake's widest span, you can cover the most water with the least amount of effort (although it may take some time to locate all the jugs in the morning).

One of Altman's favorite jugging areas is a creek arm directly off the main lake. "I like to find a long creek arm with a relatively deep, distinct channel running through it. Ideally, I prefer the wind to be blowing directly into the arm. When I set the jugs, I scatter them at 10- to 30-yard intervals across the creek mouth, letting the wind blow them up the creek." This tactic not only lets his bait cover various depths and structure, but the jugs move into a more confined area where they are more easily found at night.

Nocturnal catfish jugging requires the use of a powerful, hand-held spotlight for locating the jugs. Altman prefers spending the

Complete Angler's Library

night jugging with a partner or two. "A buddy not only makes the trip a lot more enjoyable, but is a help in dropping and locating the jugs, as well as chasing down those jugs being carried away by big cats. When we start looking for jugs, one of us operates the boat's outboard (at idle speed) while the other sits up front, scanning the water with the spotlight for fugitive jugs and renegade cats. Then when we approach a jug, we kill the outboard. The person in the bow then uses the electric trolling motor to close in on the jug."

When a catfish is hooked, it usually swims away with the jug in tow. "We use a strong electric motor in chasing cats. Still, a catfish of any size is very difficult to run down. Usually when you begin easing the boat near the jug, the cat makes a sudden dive and pulls the jug underwater. Then the jug emerges a few moments later a hundred yards or so away from the boat. On a good night, you spend most of your time chasing cats," Altman says, "and the sun peeks over the horizon before you know it."

Altman suggests not wrapping the jug's line around your hand when retrieving a cat. "A big catfish won't feel very heavy when you pick up the jug," he says, "but you're likely to go swimming if he makes a run and you get your hand tangled in the line. Whenever you pick up a jug, retrieve the line gently with your fingertips so you can drop it if a big cat suddenly takes off."

When your jug fishing is done, retrieve all your jugs and take them home with you. If you do not want to save them for later use, please dispose of them properly.

10

Allegheny Catfish King

by Mike Bleech

Nothing pleases Jim Rogers more than watching someone's face light up the night they hook their first flathead catfish. That's how we met. Jim offered to introduce a mutual friend to flatheads, and I was invited along. Though Jim's catfishing expertise is legendary along the Allegheny River of northwestern Pennsylvania, his methods are not secrets. He has shared them with many folks.

That first night spent with Jim on the river was the start of several successful flathead-fishing excursions. Hooking a flathead (I caught the first one) is an experience similar to hooking a bowling ball that is rolling downstairs. This demonstrates one of several reasons why flatheads are seldom caught. Few anglers on the Allegheny River use tackle stout enough to do battle with flatheads.

Before, I had been merely curious about a mystery fish and about a guy with a reputation for being the best at catching it. After that first flathead, however, I became a serious student of professor Jim's school of flathead catfishing.

Jim is best known as the angler who caught the Pennsylvania record channel catfish; however, he says that the catch was an accident. He was fishing for flatheads at the time. In all of the years he has fished for flatheads, he has caught only a very few channel cats.

"I don't know why," Jim says, "but 95 percent of the catfish you catch out of this part of the river are flatheads." Jim caught

Flatheads like these are a favorite target in Pennsylvania's Allegheny River; however, the successful fishermen use stout rods and tackles because catching a flathead is like catching a bowling ball rolling downstairs.

the 35-pound, record channel cat from the Allegheny River in 1970 in a pool just upriver from Oil City.

We were fishing just 300 yards upriver from the spot where Jim caught the record channel cat, "The only reason I was down there was because there was someone here," he says.

Flatheads still are Jim's favorite quarry, though. Now retired, he learned about Allegheny River flatheads from his father when Jim was a boy. It's a system refined by nearly a century of dedicated flathead catfishing. Yet, like so many of the best fishing systems, it sounds (and is) very simple.

Flatheads remain a mystery to most anglers who fish the Allegheny. Even though Jim's system is simple, it is the best way to catch flatheads in this kind of water. If you don't take all the key steps, you will almost surely fail. The system is based on timing, location and technique, all of which result from Jim's knowledge about this unusual gamefish.

Flatheads are one of two giant North American catfish species (blues are the other) that can reach a maximum size of well over 100 pounds. The Pennsylvania sportfishing record flathead weighed 43 pounds, 9 ounces. Jim's biggest cat weighed 37 pounds and measured 44 inches in length. Most run 6 to 8 pounds. "I've caught dozens of them that would go 28, 29 pounds," Jim says. Most anglers expect flatheads to behave like their smaller bullhead cousins, wallowing in muddy bottoms in still waters and eating smelly carrion. But, in reality, flathead cats eat living flesh. Their habitat is rock-bottom river channels in moderate current.

"These catfish like the current. They aren't like the catfish in stagnant water, like the catfish in the South that you read about," Jim explains. "They're more like trout or walleyes."

The river pool at Walnut Bend (Jim's boyhood home) is one of the better flathead pools, although not many big flatheads are caught there. Others are Rockmere Eddy (in the middle Allegheny), Oleopolis, Henry's Bend, Trunkeyville, President and Kennerdell. The upper limit of the best flathead water in the river is in Forest County. Flatheads get increasingly abundant downriver toward the Kennerdell area. "From here, at Rockmere, down to Kennerdell is my favorite stretch," Jim says. "You can fish anywhere here."

The river's nature changes upriver from Forest County—not so much on the surface, but significantly underwater. Upriver

Big flatheads seem to prefer the deep water in pools within the river. In fact, deep water seems to be an important element for flatheads. Rocks are another big factor.

from Forest County the overall depth is shallower with not much water deeper than 10 feet. The exception is a few places where the river was dredged for gravel. Flatheads are caught regularly in these dredge pools, but the fishing is not nearly as good as downriver. Downriver, pools are longer and deeper. One productive stretch that I charted with sonar was 20 to 30 feet deep for several hundred yards.

Deep water seems to be one of the most important elements for flatheads. Few flatheads are found in pools less than 10 feet deep. A strong relationship exists between depth and the extent of deep water in a pool and the size of the flatheads inhabiting that pool. Flatheads weighing 20 pounds and more are almost always caught in pools, having some water at least 15 feet deep.

However, having said that, one would have to add that big flatheads are not always in deep water. Using a spotlight, Jim has seen big flatheads in the shallow riffles of the river.

Another important element of the better flathead pools is boulders. "See that overhanging rock?" Jim asked, while we fished Rockmere Eddy. He was pointing toward a huge boulder that hung about 5 feet over the river. "Many times we have pulled the

Allegheny Catfish King   113

Working Boulders For Flatheads

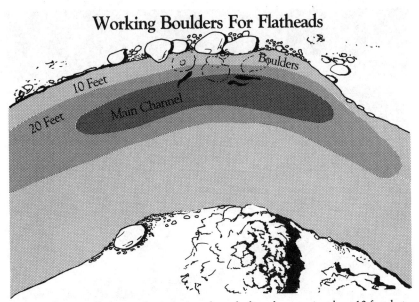

Rogers will position his boat in the main river channel where the water is at least 10 feet deep, and over submerged boulders. He believes flatheads seek refuge in the boulders when they're not active and out in the channel feeding.

boat under it to get out of the rain." Boulders like that one were scattered along the river bank—some partly submerged—near each of the pools where we caught flatheads.

"My dad said the flatheads hide under the boulders during the day," Jim explained. "It makes sense, because the lines set closest to the boulders often are the first ones hit."

This is another example of the knowledge Jim has acquired about river and flathead fishing over the years. Much of what he has learned is as applicable today as it was then. The most dramatic change that has occurred is how Jim gets about from hotspot to hotspot on the river.

His most sophisticated piece of flathead fishing gear is an 18-foot, flat-bottom, aluminum boat powered by a jet-drive, 70-horsepower outboard motor. While certainly not a necessity for flathead catfishing, this river rig is roomy and comfortable, and best of all is its ability to operate in shallow water. While even small propeller-driven boats require a couple feet of water, the jet drive will operate in 6 inches of water.

Access can be a problem when you're flathead fishing on the Allegheny because shallow, boulder-strewn riffles separate many of the best pools. Navigating through these shallows with standard propeller-driven motors is too difficult while the river is at its normal, low flow during the summer. And attempting it at night is foolhardy. But now that jet-drive outboard motors are more easily attainable, the possibility of locating new flathead water becomes inviting for more anglers. One of Jim's goals is to explore pools in the remotest part of the river, above Kennerdell.

With the exception of his jet boat, Jim's flathead fishing gear is crude in comparison with most modern tackle; yet, it all has a purpose and is hard to improve upon. It seems more appropriate on an ocean-going fishing boat than on a freshwater riverboat. The reels are old Ocean City revolving spools, without levelwinds. The rods are stiff, solid glass with long handles. The line is 150-pound test, braided nylon.

The reel is a key piece, and it should have a clicker which can be engaged while the reel is in the free-spool mode. Flatheads run with a bait, so you must let them take line before setting the hook. The clicker alerts you to the run, which is difficult to detect in the dark. It also prevents over-runs that may occur when the cat peels out line. Without the reel being set in free-spool, you would not

While Jim Rogers has simple tastes as far as tackle is concerned, he wants the best for a fishing platform. This jet boat gives him access to some shallow areas that he couldn't enter with a conventional motor.

have time to pay out line when a flathead takes the bait. You might not even have time to grab your outfit before it goes into the river. Jim said the 150-pound-test line was the only heavy line available when he needed it. He considers 50-pound-test line adequate, but just barely. Heavier line does not bother the flatheads. Some anglers question the need for such heavy tackle until they tangle with their first flathead.

Another reason for the heavy tackle is that Jim is after big flatheads. He believes that flatheads travel in schools because the action often comes in flurries. Therefore, he tries to boat each fish as quickly as possible. With light tackle, one modest-sized flathead might tie you up until the school moves out or the flatheads quit feeding. By boating each fish as quickly as possible, he greatly improves his odds of hooking a giant catfish.

Jim is fussy about his bait. He only uses chubs, which he catches from a creek that flows into the river. He wants chubs at least 4 inches long, but no longer than 7 inches. Jim misses too many hits when he uses baits larger than that, although a big flathead could certainly swallow a much larger fish. "My father tried two hooks with corn or stinkbait on one hook and a chub on the other. They never failed to take the chub."

Stinkbaits and chicken parts, reputed to be great catfish baits in some areas, catch nothing but mud turtles, hellbenders and mud puppies here. Other small fish do not get the job done, either. Crayfish should be good bait, Jim says, because most of the flatheads he has cleaned had crayfish in their bellies. But crayfish do not struggle enough when they're hooked as bait.

The chubs that Jim uses are very active. Anytime I touched the line I felt them struggling on the hooks, sending out vibrations that almost certainly would attract flatheads. You have the right chubs if they make a racket and are hard to catch inside your bait bucket and if they try to jump out of the bucket whenever you open the lid.

Jim's terminal rig consists of a ¾-ounce sinker at the line's end and two large hooks on short leaders. Chubs are hooked through the lips.

"That is just the way I was taught to rig, and I never changed," Jim says. The heavy sinker is necessary to keep the baits on the bottom. If the baits drift with the current, they will usually snag on the rocky bottoms that flatheads prefer. Flatheads do not seem

Terminal Rig For Flathead Catfish

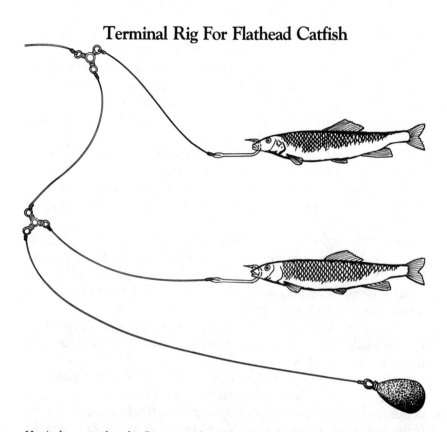

Here's the terminal rig that Rogers uses for catching flatheads. The main line and leaders are both at least 50-pound test, attesting to Rogers' belief in stout tackle for flatheads.

to mind carrying the heavy sinker.

Two hooks are attached to the main line by 10- to 12-inch leaders clipped from the main line. The hooks should be large enough so that the gap is greater than the thickness of the chub's head. This will decrease the likelihood of the hook point burying in the bait instead of the catfish when you set the hook. Jim is not fussy about hook size, as long as it is big enough, nor is he fussy about its style. "It is hard to find big enough hooks around here," Jim says. "You have to take whatever you can get." Two chubs are better than one because they cause twice as much disturbance.

In some other places, under different conditions, flatheads might possibly be caught during the day. But not on the Allegheny. Here it is a nighttime game. The best time is June through September, peaking in August. However, May and October also can be good some years. And not all nights are good during the peak months. Jim uses the moon to pattern his flathead fishing.

"The last quarter and the new moon are the best times," he explains. "The new moon is best, but the last quarter is good, too. For every one you get when the moon is shining brightly, you will get eight or 10 when it is blocked by clouds, only partially lighted or not seen. Moonless nights are best." In fact, Jim doesn't fish for flatheads at any other times than during these peak periods because of the vast difference in fishing success.

Jim has found that a light rain or drizzle increases the action. However, hard, long rains that roil and raise the river typically hurt flathead fishing.

Artificial light is also an important negative factor. "If you're catching them and someone has a bright light shining along shore, they'll quit instantly," Jim says. "My dad would yell, 'Turn that light out!' if someone turned on a porch light at a camp along shore. But I don't say anything."

That explains the lack of success by anglers who keep a lantern lit while fishing. Jim uses a flashlight, but he's careful to keep the light inside the boat.

Low, normal summertime river flow of clear water (without floating weeds) is the ideal condition. Contrary to what is said about flathead fishing in some other rivers, Jim has not found the fishing good in muddy water. Floating weeds are a big headache because they catch on the line and slide down to the baits. Rigs must be checked frequently and cleared of weeds.

Jim gets his boat into position before nightfall; navigating the boat is easier and safer during daylight. Once on the pool that he intends to fish, he drifts the boat into position over the main river channel.

"Watch for the foam line," Jim explains. "The foam floats right over the deepest part of the river channel." Jim fishes in the pool's main current, but not where the current is swiftest. This is generally in the pool's broad center over deep water. Jim usually doesn't use his sonar because he has learned the locations for the best fishing. The rest of us, however, would probably be much better off using sonar to locate the pool's deeper parts and the underwater boulders.

Anchors on equal length ropes at each end of the boat are used to position the boat sideways in the current. This is so three anglers can each spread two rigs without tangling. One way Jim determines whether the current is right for flathead fishing is in picking a spot where the boat can be safely anchored sideways. This method can be dangerous in smaller boats, which should be anchored from the bow only so the bow faces into the current.

On this particular night, the flatheads began hitting soon after sundown, even though there was still some light in the sky. That was one of the better nights, even though the action ceased quite early. Most nights it is dark for a while before the activity begins. During the peak month, August, the best fishing is usually from 9 p.m. until midnight. Most of the action is from 9 until 11, but most flatheads are in the 5- to 10-pound range.

"I don't think I have ever caught one over 15 pounds before 10, 11 o'clock," Jim says. Bigger ones always seem to bite later. From 11 until 2 is when you catch the big ones."

Most nights you sit for a long time before the first pickup. Your mind wanders, and perhaps you doze. Then the clicker begins to sing, bringing you back to consciousness. Let the flathead run with the bait for a while. If it stops, wait. Don't try to set the hook until it runs again. Then lean back and hang on!

Walleyes

11

River Walleyes

by Chris Niskanen

D ave Lincoln's life, in many ways, has been connected to river walleye fishing. One of the Midwest's finest walleye rivers—the Mississippi—makes a graceful turn along the eastern boundary of Lincoln's hometown of Dubuque, Iowa. And for 17 years, Lincoln was co-owner of a sporting goods department at a local hardware store, selling fishing tackle to area walleye gurus and learning their secrets.

"It's funny, I always did more bass fishing," says Lincoln, who recently opened his own tackle store. "I fished bass tournaments for 10 years, but I also really loved jigging for walleyes."

Lincoln has turned serious attention to river-walleye fishing. He teamed up with one of those local walleye gurus, Art Lehrman, and they hit the Masters Walleye Circuit when MWC officials began holding tournaments in Dubuque. Unknown on the circuit, the Iowans soon established themselves as two of the Midwest's best walleye anglers.

In two years, Lincoln and Lehrman became one of the premier teams on the tourney trail, winning the MWC's World Championship in 1990 and missing "team of the year" honors by a few points. In their first MWC tournament of 1991, they took second place on the Illinois River, showing that their success the previous year was no fluke.

River Experts
While they also have proven their mettle on lakes, Lincoln

As a team, Lincoln and Lehrman have made a name for themselves in walleye circles by not following the crowd. They've discovered areas in rivers that aren't usually fished by serious walleye anglers.

River Walleyes

and Lehrman are best known for their knowledge of river walleye fishing. Basically, Lincoln and Lehrman have found success by finding walleyes in places that other anglers have overlooked.

"Art likes to fish by himself," Lincoln explains. "Even if we know there is a concentration of fish and we need fish, he won't go there if there are other people there."

That tenacity for finding fish away from the crowds has made Lincoln and Lehrman somewhat of an enigma on the Masters Walleye Circuit. Rivers are dynamic systems, presenting anglers with many conditions and locations for finding walleyes. Walleyes are the river's nomads, migrating on a seasonal basis from different habitats searching for prey.

So when tournament anglers find walleyes on a river, it's not uncommon to find 30 or more boats fishing one area. But you won't find Lincoln or Lehrman among them.

As a team, Lincoln says they fish river riprap and wing-dam structure that is well-known among river walleye anglers. But they also have discovered something called "submerged bank protection," a type of structure that has always been in the river but is new territory in walleye fishing circles. Unless an angler has done some homework, he would have no reason to know it is there.

Lincoln says the best times to fish these three areas—riprap, wing dams and submerged bank protection—depend upon the season. Of course, there are different techniques for fishing each type of structure. And no one masters river fishing for walleyes on one trip. It takes practice—lots of practice.

Spring And Summer Fishing

In the springtime, Lincoln puts his boat in the Mississippi River as soon as there is open water—even if it means bumping a few floating ice chunks. Spring walleyes are searching for spawning areas, and one of the most popular areas to fish are tailwaters below dams.

While many anglers dodge each other in the dam tailwaters, Lincoln and Lehrman cast small jigs along downstream riprapped shorelines, where walleyes also spawn.

"We don't even go close to tailwaters anymore because everyone else is there," Lincoln says. "You can also get bigger fish downstream. Riprap is one of our favorite spots. We'll be fishing very shallow, from 6 to 8 feet."

Fishing Creek Mouths For Walleyes

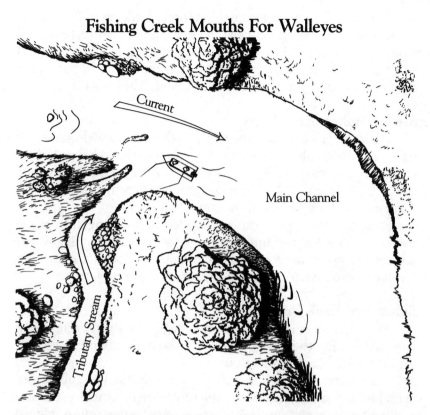

One place where you'll find Lincoln and Lehrman is at the mouths of feeder creeks. These small rivers or creeks that flow into the main river are frequently overlooked walleye hangouts.

The pair doesn't anchor but moves constantly, casting plastics with small jigs or jigs tipped with minnows.

Often the anglers vertically jig while working upstream using a bow-mounted trolling motor. This technique won Lincoln and Lehrman second place in the Illinois River tournament. They would work ⅛- to ⅜-ounce, blue-colored jigs tipped with minnows vertically.

Creek Mouths

In addition to riprapped shorelines, creek mouths are effective areas to fish in the spring. Creeks that feed major rivers like the Mississippi are a fine source of aquatic nutrients, which in turn attract baitfish. While river walleyes do not travel far up creeks, they often congregate near creek mouths to feed. Creeks also provide eddies and other structure that protect walleyes from current.

Lincoln pointed to Catfish Creek, a stream near Dubuque, as a perfect example. "At Catfish Creek, there is a wide river bend that offers protection so the fish don't get blown out by the river's current," he says. "But most of all, the creek holds baitfish."

Scents And Stinger Hooks

Their secret weapon in the spring is the use of a wide variety of fish scents. Lincoln says scents give cold-water walleyes a little more incentive to take jigs. "It's a major factor when the water is cold," Lincoln says. "We'll use four or five different kinds. In tournaments, we'll use them all the time."

Stinger hooks are another must for light-biting springtime walleyes. "A lot of the time a walleye just smacks the jig. When you set the hook, all you get back is a minnow with a scuffed up tail," Lincoln says. A stinger hook solves that problem.

Submerged Bank Protection

As the water warms and summer begins, walleyes migrate to wing dams and other rocky areas near the main channel, including submerged bank protection.

Most river anglers know about wing dams, but submerged bank protection may be still completely foreign. Lincoln says submerged bank protection is essentially underwater riprap, placed along river bends and straight shorelines by the U.S. Army Corps of Engineers to prevent erosion. Because it's submerged, it's not easy to find.

"It can be near the middle of the river," Lincoln says, "and you have to use electronics to find it. And not all bank protection is created equal."

Owning a good river map, such as the Mississippi River navigation charts published by the U.S. Corps of Engineers, is a major advantage for finding good submerged bank protection. Quizzing local anglers and Corps workers can also narrow your search for this special walleye hangout.

Once it is found, any variety of lures can be used to catch walleyes on submerged bank protection. "We'll jig-fish it, use three-way rigs and troll and throw crankbaits," Lincoln says. And submerged bank protection holds fish all summer long and well into the fall.

Fishing Submerged Bank Protection, Wing Dams

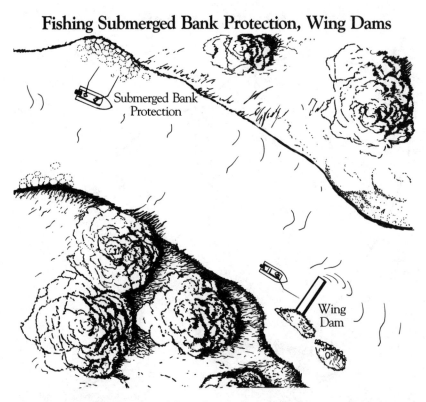

Submerged Bank Protection

Wing Dam

The Iowans also will be found carefully working the face of wing dams, as well as submerged bank protection. Submerged bank protection has always been in rivers like the Mississippi, but few anglers have discovered its location.

Fishing The Three-Way Rig

When he is not fishing submerged bank protection, Lincoln trolls the upstream-faces of wing dams for summer and fall walleyes.

Their most common setup is a three-way rig. It involves a 12- to 15-inch dropline from the bottom of the three-way swivel and a 3-to 4-foot leader from the top.

Lincoln has numerous ways of baiting the leader of three-way rigs, including live bait and crankbaits. The type of weight on the dropline depends upon what is on the leader. If he is using live bait, he often uses a jig-shad body combination on the dropline. If a crankbait is tied to the leader, he uses a bell sinker.

Crankbaits are an effective lure for use on three-way rigs. "We'll use crankbaits on wing dams as early as possible in the sum-

Basic Three-Way Rig

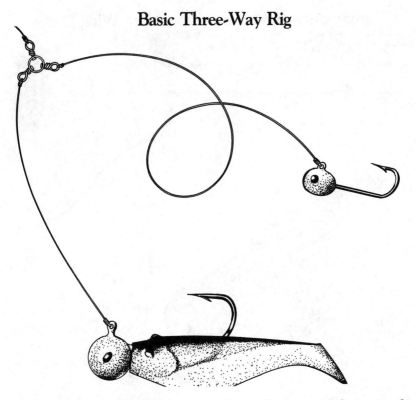

This angling team uses a basic three-way rig, making modifications to suit the situation. One version is a plain jig and a hook tipped with plastic, or just a plain hook, or a crankbait and a weight. The type of weight depends upon the bait selected.

mer," Lincoln says. When using a crankbait, he prefers No. 7 or No. 9 Rapalas, either orange or chartreuse. Crayfish-colored crankbaits are effective in late summer months.

While others often alter treble hooks on crankbaits, such as removing one hook to reduce snagging, Lincoln leaves them alone. "They are fine just the way they come," he says.

When using live bait, Lincoln tips the leaders with night-crawlers or leeches about 90 percent of the time. Here, the effective combinations are a floating jig tipped with a nightcrawler or leech, or a plain, No. 4 Tru-turn hook baited with either a leech or nightcrawler.

Often, Lincoln uses beads or spinners ahead of a nightcrawler to make it more enticing. Beads and spinners draw a walleye's attention to the nightcrawler, one of Lincoln's prime baits.

"If you want to use live bait, nothing can beat the old night-crawler for walleye fishing," Lincoln says.

Leeches are relatively new on the live-bait scene for Mississippi River fishermen in Iowa. They have been so successful that anglers want them in the spring as soon as they can be shipped to bait shops from Minnesota and Wisconsin. "Leeches have done so well everywhere else, people around here just said, 'Why not?'" Lincoln says.

So what does he prefer, a leech or a nightcrawler?

"I'd probably pick a leech over a nightcrawler," he says, "but Art would probably pick a nightcrawler."

Trolling a three-way rig with live bait across a wing-dam face isn't as easy as it sounds. Lincoln says it was the most difficult river-walleye fishing technique he had to master.

"It took me a long time to get the hang of it," he says. "Art used to take me out and make sure that I would get into some fish. It took me about half a season to learn it."

The trick is telling the difference between a walleye strike and simply the rig's bounce on the bottom. A walleye doesn't always hit a live-bait rig as hard as a crankbait. Of course, it's something that can't be learned by reading. Like other types of river-walleye fishing, it takes practice—lots of practice.

Boat Control

Good boat control is essential for fishing wing dams. Lincoln credits his partner, Art Lehrman, for possessing perhaps the best boat-control skills of any river angler.

When they fish together, Lehrman always operates that bow-mounted electric trolling motor while Lincoln fishes from the boat's rear. "Art always knows where the boat is and where everything else is," Lincoln says. "He pinpoints the place where we should fish."

Thus, it naturally follows that the trick to good boat control is not only knowing how to maneuver the boat, but knowing the specific structure of a wing dam—how big it is, where there are breaks in it and where there are crevices and nooks.

"Practice is the name of the game," Lincoln says. "When Art first started fishing, he used a couple of 2-ounce sinkers tied on a line. He would work wing dams with the weights to learn how to fish it."

If there is one key piece of equipment in Lehrman's and Lincoln's fishing system, it would be the electric trolling motor. They would not be able to work wing dams the way they do without it.

Every wing dam is different, with a different current flow and configuration. Using his sinker method, Lehrman discovered the structure of his favorite wing dams—places where some rocks stuck out and others where rocks had washed away.

Fishing With Jigs And Plastics

You probably won't find a river walleye angler more devoted to jigs and plastics than Dave Lincoln (except his partner, Art Lehrman).

"I think we probably broke new ground by using more and more plastics on the river," Lincoln says. "There are not many guys who fish an eight-hour tournament using only plastics. Plastics work year-round. A lot of times in tournaments, Art starts by using plastics and I begin with live bait. Rarely does the live bait

Complete Angler's Library

work better than the plastic in taking fish."

That may seem like an odd statement to die-hard river fishermen who rarely use anything but a jig-and-minnow combination. But Lincoln and Lehrman have spent thousands of hours perfecting the right presentations using plastics and jigs.

Their favorite plastic-jig combination is a plastic shad body on a jig, a combination that Lincoln calls "matching the hatch."

"There are a zillion shad in the river," Lincoln says. "Fish see the body shape and the shine of the plastic shad body, and that's what they snap at. That is what really matches the hatch."

Lincoln says the shad body was discovered by Lehrman, who purchased several of the lures at Lincoln's store. After his first fishing trip with them, Lehrman gave them rave reviews.

"We once ran the boat all the way up to Guttenberg, Iowa, and hit every wing dam on our way down the river," Lincoln recalls. "I think we caught walleyes on every wing dam using shad bodies. It was crazy. Sometimes we even had doubles on."

The combination of a jig and shad body is now one of their most successful rigs. Lincoln recommends using the 2½-inch bodies for ⅛- and ¼-ounce jigs; with larger jigs, they'll use the 3-inch bodies.

Their favorite shad is tinted pearl blue with a black stripe on the back. While there are other colors and styles of shad bodies, none is as effective as the tinted pearl-blue variety, Lincoln says.

Selection of a shad body size also depends upon the season. "In the springtime, you'll want to use the 3-inch size because the shad left over from the winter are all big," Lincoln says. "As the season progresses, you revert to the smaller ones."

When fishing jigs with plastic shad bodies or the traditional curlytail, Lincoln believes lighter jigs are always best. Inexperienced river walleye anglers always use a heavy jig to keep in constant touch with the bottom—no matter how strong the current.

"On about every third bounce, you'll get snagged," Lincoln says. "You want to go as light as you can and still keep in the fish zone as much as you can. Many times you feel it bouncing along the rocks, but (the jig) still isn't heavy enough to get snagged."

Of course, you won't always be able to use ¼-ounce jigs on every wing dam. This is because of strong currents.

"But on the wing dams where you can get away with a quarter ounce, then use a quarter ounce," Lincoln recommends. He believes river anglers should use the lightest jigs possible.

Lincoln's preferred jig colors are a two-toned chartreuse and orange, blue, plain orange, plain chartreuse and pink.

When he is not using a shad body, Lincoln uses a jig-and-curly-tail combination. His favorite curlytail colors are motor oil, chartreuse and fire cracker.

Fall Fishing

"With winter coming, walleyes become more ferocious feeders," Lincoln says, "and life for fishermen gets a whole lot easier. The walleyes start showing up in good numbers. That's when you wonder where they were all summer long."

During a Masters Walleye Circuit tournament, which Lincoln and Lehrman won on the Mississippi River in Red Wing, Minnesota, they learned how finicky river walleyes can be.

"We were up there all week and never found fish until the last day," Lincoln recalls. "We just fished sand bars on Lake Pepin's points, and we finally found one that no one else was fishing.

"I was using mostly live bait, while Art was switching back and forth between live bait and plastics. He eventually caught an 8- and 7-pounder with plastics, and I caught a 4-pounder on a Fireball jig and a minnow. We caught those fish in about 20 minutes." The team put together a two-day total of 38.6 pounds, outdistancing the second-place team by a mere pound.

Under normal conditions, Lincoln and Lehrman fish the same structure in fall (submerged bank protection and wing dams) as in summer. Shad bodies are very effective because walleyes are beginning to gorge heavily on their favorite food fish.

Rods, Reels And Line

Rods and reels for river walleyes depend upon the kind of weight and rig used, Lincoln says. With lightweight jigs ($\frac{1}{16}$ ounce to $\frac{1}{4}$ ounce), he uses a medium-length spinning rod-and-reel combination. For heavier jigs, a casting rod is more effective. When using three-way rigs, Lincoln says he always uses a casting rod.

When fishing lighter jigs, Lincoln will use 8-pound-test line. With heavier jigs, he'll move up to 10-pound line.

River Levels

Fluctuating river levels can play havoc on walleyes and an angler's ability to catch them. "A lot of it depends upon how drastic the river has changed," Lincoln says. "I'd rather not fish a river that is going down; either way, though, it's not worth a darn if it's a drastic change. If you are going to have a subtle change, I'd rather have the river coming up just a bit. It doesn't seem to bother the fish as much."

The key to fishing a fluctuating river is to fish shallow. "If the river is coming up real quick," Lincoln says, "Art and I fish shallow. If it's dropping, we also go shallow, but not as much. When it's dropping, you would think the fish would move out where it's deeper, but they really don't. They'll stay in the same place, only in a little shallower water."

Future Of River Walleye Fishing

Lincoln says the future of river walleye fishing will involve finding and catching fish in non-traditional areas, such as backwater sloughs. Some anglers have successfully caught fish (and won tournaments) by catching springtime spawning walleyes in backwater sloughs; however, it's a hit-and-miss situation. "We can't get anything constant in backwater sloughs," Lincoln says.

Someday anglers will learn how to catch walleyes in cattail beds, Lincoln says. "We once caught some saugers in a running chute near coontails," he says. "But it's something that doesn't last very long."

One thing is certain: Research by state fishery biologists continues to reveal new secrets for catching river walleyes. Lincoln says he and Lehrman have talked to several local biologists about their research on walleye migratory movements and other walleye habitats and fisheries. "Most people never realize how many fish there are in the rivers," Lincoln says.

=========12=========

Night-Shift Walleyes

======= by Mark Romanack =======

W
hen it's time for second-shift workers to punch out for the day, a Michigan-based angler punches in for another evening of trophy walleye fishing. A respected guide and tournament professional, Tom Irwin makes a living from catching graveyard-shift walleyes that others ignore.

A full-time fishing guide, Irwin has recently started fishing the walleye tournament circuit. Irwin and his fishing partner, Dr. Steven Holt, have previously qualified for the coveted Masters Walleye Circuit World Championship. During one tournament season, they finished eighth overall and recorded some of the heaviest tournament weights at several events.

Staying out all night has gotten Irwin into a lot of fights—the kind anglers dream about. A dedicated night troller, Irwin wrestles with more than his share of trophy walleyes each year. In an average season, Irwin guides his clients to 20 or more walleyes larger than 8 pounds.

Why Fish At Night?

Fishing by starlight appeals to some anglers, but most shy away from the water once the sun goes down. "Fishing at night takes more effort and advance planning, but there's no better time to fish for trophy walleyes," says Irwin. "When the sun sets, monster walleyes go on the prowl in search of baitfish that are almost helpless against these efficient predators."

Tom Irwin is hooked on nightfishing because that's when the big walleyes go prowling for food. Catches like this are routine for Irwin, a dedicated night-troller.

Night-Shift Walleyes

Walleyes claim a distinct hunting advantage after dark. The large, light-gathering qualities of a walleye's eyes enable it to see better than forage fish in low light. Walleyes also have a highly developed lateral-line sense that helps them hone in on baitfish.

The lateral line is a sensory organ that interprets vibrations in the water. Like a radar screen, the lateral line is an early warning system that helps walleyes track down their prey and steer clear of larger predators when visibility is limited.

"Walleyes feed actively at night because it requires less energy for them to catch food than during the day," explains Irwin. "Under the cover of darkness, walleyes cruise along drop-offs, weed edges, sunken timber and other cover or structure picking off baitfish that are nearly blind and helpless to escape. That's not to say these same fish don't feed during the day. As capable predators, walleyes will feed at any time of day or night, but they are more efficient hunters after dark."

Finding Dependable Night Bites
The nighttime walleye bite is a common phenomenon that anglers can tap into throughout the nation. Although walleyes can be caught after dark in almost any waters, certain fisheries are better for nightfishing than others.

"Strangely enough, lakes, rivers and reservoirs that provide dependable daylight bites aren't always the best nightfishing waters," Irwin says. "Typically, these fisheries contain huge numbers of baitfish, and walleyes have no problem finding enough to eat. Fishing after dark doesn't necessarily increase your odds of catching fish on this type of water."

Bodies of water that are subjected to many daytime recreational activities such as water-skiing or powerboating are excellent nighttime fishing prospects. During the summer months, the only time many of these waters are tranquil enough for walleyes to feed freely is after dark.

Natural lakes with lots of weed cover or sunken timber are also good prospects for nightfishing. "The heavy cover provides baitfish with a maze of escape routes," says Irwin. "During daylight, walleyes instinctively know that they're no match for darting baitfish and young panfish. Once darkness arrives, the tide is turned and walleyes put their nocturnal hunting advantage into effect."

Bodies of exceptionally clear water are good candidates for nightfishing tactics for walleyes. Walleyes in these waters often are reluctant to feed during the day, but really prowl at night.

Fisheries that feature exceptionally clear waters are also good candidates for nightfishing. "Super-clear water tends to make walleyes somewhat reluctant to feed actively during the day," explains Irwin. "The Sturgeon Bay area of Green Bay (on Lake Michigan) is a prime example of a clearwater nightfishery. The water in Sturgeon Bay is so clear it's tough to approach these fish during the day without spooking them. At night, this fishery absolutely explodes with angling opportunities."

Little Bay de Noc in Michigan's Upper Peninsula, Lake Erie's eastern basin, Lake Oahe in South Dakota and Lake McConoughy in Nebraska are just a few more examples of clearwater fisheries that support fantastic nightfishing opportunities. No matter where you fish for walleyes, opportunities for nighttime walleyes exist.

High Percentage Spots

As previously mentioned, nightfishing requires more advance planning than similar daytime efforts. "Before I fish any body of water after dark," Irwin says, "I check out the fishery during the day. Go slow when exploring new or unfamiliar fishing waters. Daytime explorations are the time to note navigation hazards, pinpoint important lake features and establish a plan of attack for subsequent nightfishing trips."

Irwin concentrates his nightfishing efforts on several different aquatic features. Natural bottom structure such as sunken islands, humps, reefs and sharply sloping breaklines attract large numbers of foraging night-bite walleyes. Also, Irwin looks for riprapped shorelines, breakwalls and pierheads when hunting for moonlight walleyes.

"Most lakes have one or more of these natural and man-made aquatic features to choose from," says Irwin. "My home water, Muskegon Lake in western Michigan, offers all of these important walleye magnets."

One of Irwin's favorite mid-lake reefs holds fish all season long. "I'll usually find walleyes on top of the reef in shallow water or cruising along the steep breakline where they pin baitfish against the bank," says Irwin. "During the day the fish stick to the nearby deep water and move shallow at night to feed. On the good nights you can actually hear walleyes splashing in the shallows as they chase down their next meal."

Like thousands of other lakes in timber country, the bottom of Muskegon Lake features several sunken woodpiles left as reminders of a logging era past. "Years ago, saw mills had no commercial use for the strips of slab wood and bark trimmed away from sawed logs," explains Irwin. "The strips of slab wood were bundled and drafted onto the ice during the winter. The spring thaws sent these wooden waste piles to the lake's bottom where they were out of sight and mind."

Out of sight, perhaps, but these sunken slab piles are seldom far from the minds of anglers who know that panfish, bass, pike and walleyes are all frequent visitors to these twisted tangles of wood and bark.

Muskegon Lake also offers its share of riprap to explore. "A channel leading out into Lake Michigan is a popular nightfishing spot," Irwin says. "Riprapped shorelines, breakwalls and pierheads are productive fish-holding structure and fairly easy to fish in the dark."

A productive fishing spot at night, riprap can be frustrating to fish during the day. "My tournament partner, Steve Holt, is an avid scuba diver," explains Irwin. "Steve has explored the riprapped Muskegon Lake channel many times during daylight to explore why these fish only seem willing to bite at night."

"Every time I've explored riprap at the channel's edge," Holt explains, "I've spotted walleyes. The fish are usually tucked back into the cracks and crevices between the rocks, like moray eels. After studying these fish, I'm convinced they're almost strictly nocturnal." The fishing situations that Irwin faces every night on Muskegon Lake are not unique to this one body of water. Hundreds of other lakes, rivers and reservoirs offer similar fishing opportunities.

Trolling Tactics

Although Irwin has mastered all the popular techniques of walleye fishing, trolling crankbaits is the primary method he uses to catch night-bite walleyes. "Walleyes become very active at night," says Irwin, "which means they're often scattered. Trolling is certainly the best way to cover water quickly while hunting for fish."

Crankbaits are the best weapons when night-trolling. "We troll cranks for several reasons," says Irwin. "Perhaps most importantly, crankbaits can be used to closely imitate the natural forage walleyes are looking for. If the lake I'm fishing has a gizzard shad forage base, crankbaits featuring a shad-like profile are the first baits I'll try. Sort of like 'matching the hatch,' cranks also offer the flexibility to fish deep or shallow."

When a crankbait passes through the water, it displaces water in much the same way as baitfish do. Even though walleyes see better than their prey after dark, their vision isn't perfect in the pre-dawn hours. "Walleyes use their lateral line to focus on vibrations given off by crankbaits," explains Irwin. "Because these lures are fairly large and armed with many razor-sharp hooks, the odds of a fish actually catching a crankbait and getting hooked are far better than with other lures."

All of Irwin's nighttime trolling is done with a powerful, yet silent, 24-volt electric motor. While walleyes are often very ac-

Trolling With Deep Divers On Short Leads

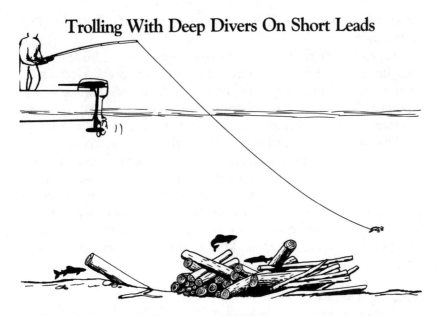

Using short leads from 40 to 60 feet, Irwin works sunken wood piles and other structure with deep-diving crankbaits. He also uses a trolling motor so he can move slowly and quietly.

tive after dark, they are also easily spooked and difficult to approach when the angler is running an outboard motor.

"It takes 24 volts of power to provide enough juice to troll all night long," says Irwin. "Even the most powerful 12-volt electric motor simply doesn't have enough thrust to push a fully loaded fishing boat for extended periods of time."

Irwin prefers to use a transom-mounted electric motor when guiding clients; however, he admits that a bow-mounted motor is a little easier to control. "I run a transom-mounted electric motor because it positions me at a better spot in the boat to help my clients," says Irwin. "When a client's rod gets tangled or snagged, I can deal with this and other problems a lot better from the back of the boat."

Most fishermen find they have better control when using a bow-mounted electric motor. If the wind picks up, a pair of anglers running transom- and bow-mounted electric motors at the same time can keep the boat under control in even very difficult conditions.

When trolling isolated cover such as slab piles or bottom structure like reefs, sunken points and islands, Irwin suggests using deep-diving crankbaits on a fairly short lead. "Deep-diving cranks offer a lot of flexibility when night-trolling," says Irwin. "Combining a deep-diving bait with a fairly short lead enables the angler to follow meandering contours more precisely and stay on top of isolated cover such as slab piles."

A lead length of 40 to 60 feet allows diving cranks to achieve most of their depth potential. Short leads also enable the angler to feel the lure's vibrating action much better than longer leads. Detecting strikes while trolling is more difficult than many anglers expect. A walleye can inhale a crankbait and swim along without the angler feeling any resistance at all. Sometimes the only tip the angler gets is when the lure's wiggling action suddenly quits. Also, short leads reduce line stretch and deliver solid hooksets.

Obviously, it's important to select a crankbait that dives deep enough to interest walleyes without going so deep it constantly hangs up on bottom. "Three factors determine how deep a crankbait will dive," says Irwin. "The size of the lure's diving lip, the diameter of the fishing line used and the length of trolling lead all influence the dive curve of crankbaits."

When Irwin and Holt first started trolling crankbaits, they had no idea how deep their favorite lures would dive. Through the years, trial and error helped them determine which baits worked best in certain situations, but they still weren't sure how deep the lures were running.

"A couple years ago Steve and I started testing the diving depth of crankbaits," says Irwin. "To test each bait we trolled them with measured lead lengths and a scuba diver observed and documented exactly how deep various baits would run. Our testing provided some surprising results, settled a few bets and confirmed many suspicions we wondered about for years."

Each time Irwin and Holt test a new bait, they document exact diving depths on various lead lengths and formulate a depth curve. The data these anglers have collected is being compiled into a book for other anglers to use and enjoy.

In the meantime, Irwin publishes a feature column known as "Crankbaits 'In Depth'" that highlights a different lure model along with its depth-curve graph each month.

Trolling Riprap
When trolling riprap or other clearly visible structure, boat

Walleye Rig For Working Riprap

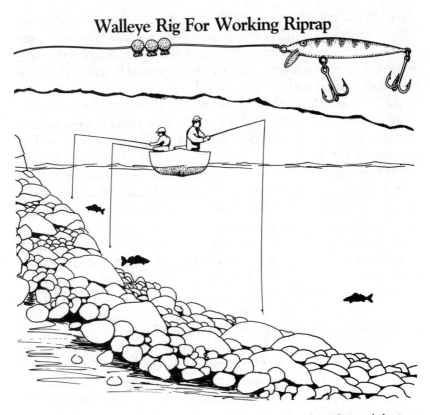

Riprap is a favorite target in walleye night-trolling. This shows how the anglers work the riprap from both sides of the boat. Shown above is one popular rig.

control isn't a problem. In these situations Irwin switches over to shallow-diving crankbaits and uses longer trolling leads to maximize diving depth.

"Large minnow-style stickbaits are my favorite night-trolling lures," says Irwin. "The bigger these baits are the better I like them. Many anglers would scoff at the idea of fishing walleyes with 8-inch-long magnum crankbaits, but I'm convinced large baits catch more and bigger fish."

To help these shallow divers achieve greater depths, Irwin frequently attaches two or three small split shots on the line a couple feet ahead of the lure. Using split shots has another advantage. When trolled, the split shots have a tendency to hang below the lure and catch bottom before the crankbait.

"When the split shots catch in the rocks," says Irwin, "I can

Trolling for walleyes at night involves a whole new set of problems, but the advantages more than outweigh the problems. A major challenge is keeping the bait from snagging in riprap.

Night-Shift Walleyes

usually free the lure by dropping my rod back and snapping the line quickly. Even if I can't pop the shot free immediately, it almost always comes free when I back up over the lure. If the lure itself catches bottom, the odds of recovering the bait are not very good."

Long rods are used for positioning outside baits away from the boat and reducing tangles. Baits that run near the riprap's edge typically feature shorter leads preventing the lure from diving too deep and snagging on the rocks. Shorter rods with longer leads are used progressively to follow along the riprap's contour into deeper water.

Fishing long leads makes it difficult to feel the lure working. Stiff-action graphite casting rods help the angler gain the maximum amount of feel, and they provide more power for driving hooks into the bony mouth of trophy walleyes.

Irwin combines stiff-action rods with a monofilament line that has very little stretch. "I'm really sold on cofilament fishing lines for all flatline-trolling," says Irwin. "Cofilament line has much less stretch than other monofilament lines. The extra sensitivity of these lines makes a big difference when feeling the fish is the difference between hooking a few or landing a limit."

Using low-stretch fishing line is a little tip that pays off in bigger catches of walleyes. Conditioning yourself to routinely pump your fishing rod while trolling is another little detail that makes a big difference.

"Pumping the rod doubles or triples your chances of catching fish," claims Irwin. "I'm constantly after my clients to keep pumping their rods. The action is a natural triggering element. Baitfish are constantly stopping, starting and darting around. Imitating this action guarantees you'll hook more fish."

Although many anglers think lure color doesn't matter after dark, Irwin says it's amazing how often color makes a difference: "I like baits that offer contrasting colors. Lures with dark backs and light sides or undersides work much better than solid-colored crankbaits. I've also noticed that on cloudy or overcast nights, fluorescent-colored baits produce best. If the moon is shining, a more natural silver/black, silver/green or silver/blue pattern produces best."

If the angler can choose the evenings he can go fishing, watching the moon phases can pay off immensely. Over the past eight

Complete Angler's Library

years, Irwin has maintained catch records for every one of his guide trips. "If I had a choice, I'd go fishing three to four days either side of a full moon," says Irwin. "Many of my best catches are taken during the full moon. The next best time to fish is one day either side of a new, first-quarter and second quarter moon."

No one can explain exactly why these moon phases seem to concentrate fish activity, but there's little doubt that this phenomenon benefits anglers. Fishing during the full-moon phase and concentrating angling efforts after dark are excellent ways to double the chances of battling trophy-class walleyes.

"I feel sorry for anglers who work nights," says Irwin. "While others are sleeping or slaving away on the graveyard shift, I'm enjoying walleye fishing at its best!"

=13=

Icing Walleyes On The Flats

by Jeff Murray

ditor Steve Pennaz, of *North American Fisherman* maga-
zine, couldn't believe his eyes. Neither could I. We were
guests of Rick Runquist, a north-central Minnesota fishing guide. Our late-February walleye trip to the ice-
bound surface of Leech Lake seemed to start out on a left foot.
Instead of drilling holes along traditional rocky points or over
sunken islands surrounded by deep water, we were camped in front
of a shoreline rimmed with bulrushes. The water wasn't any deeper
than 5 feet. When we stooped over our ice holes and blocked
out the sun, we could see our jigs against the sandy bottom.

But that's not all we saw on this trip. We saw and caught
walleyes in areas anglers were told to avoid: shallow flats.
Runquist is a master of the flat zone, and he's perfected several
techniques that make this fishery probably the most productive
under the ice.

But first, a crash course on winter walleye biology. Without
this perspective, the necessary subtleties and fine points of
Runquist's system seem irrelevant.

Winter Walleye Biology

For starters, all fish are ectothermic, or cold-blooded. Practically, this means that their body temperature is related to their
environment. After ice-up, walleyes adapt to uniformly cold temperatures by making certain biochemical and physiological adjustments. One such natural adjustment that ice anglers are well aware

Rick Runquist has discovered that winter walleyes will hang out in the shallow flats. In fact, Runquist has become a master of fishing these flats which have been traditionally overlooked by walleye anglers.

Icing Walleyes On The Flats

of is the walleye's lowered metabolic rate and slower movement.

No question, cold-water fish feed less often and consume less when they decide to eat. Also, their reaction time to various stimuli is slower. Furthermore, dexterity is hampered in cold, dense water because it takes greater effort to hunt down baitfish. The bottom line? Fish aren't as active as they were last summer, and anglers must adjust if they intend to score under the ice with any consistency.

Despite these severe limitations, however, walleyes do have a decided visual advantage come ice-up. Their tapetum lucidum, a mirror-like reflective tissue, returns light back into their eyes, enabling them to hunt rather effectively in dim light under ice.

When a lake is covered with ice, its water clarity undergoes a subtle change. Waves cease and currents, aided by thermal convection, are negligible. As a result, suspended particles settle out. This creates an environment that's somewhat darker, but at the same time clearer with very distinct shadows. This impacts practical lure presentations.

What about fish location? Often overlooked in winter are oxygen levels. They're generally lower but can vary noticeably in a water body. This can affect the distribution of fish.

Briefly, the main source of oxygen replenishment in a lake is plant photosynthesis. Under an icecap this is limited to the shallower zones, because the ice restricts light penetration beyond a certain depth. So it's no wonder fish typically avoid deeper water as the season progresses.

Okay, what about presentations? Because we can't troll or cast, we must closely examine lure choice and lure action. Seemingly inconsequential refinements really add up.

To begin with, we should appeal to the senses that fish rely on most heavily during cold-water periods. For example, many authorities consider the fish's lateral-line sensory system to be secondary to sight because water clarity is at a seasonal high; fish see better, so they make better use of their vision.

Moreover, scent is probably secondary to taste, which is a function of texture. Recall that cold water is denser than warm water, and currents are reduced. The chemical field surrounding a source of scent is subsequently limited to a rather small area. Add these all up, and winter fish will mouth baits. (Another subtle factor to keep in mind when considering winter presentations.)

Following Walleyes Through The Winter

Following ice-up walleyes on the flats are most apt to be found at A, the deepest part of the gradually rising flat. By mid-winter the walleyes will have spread to point B and, finally, in late season to along the shallowest part of the flat (C).

One last item is "fish activity centers." A telemetry-tracking study spearheaded by WDNR fisheries biologist Skip Sommerfeldt in north-central Wisconsin revealed that walleyes are more active in some places than others. Indeed, the fish appeared to use "resting areas" that were separate and distinct from their "feeding areas." Drilling holes on top of—or surrounding—resting fish proved futile; they were easily spooked if they weren't active. The bottom line is that even though walleyes may snack just about anywhere, they prefer to do most of their dining in well-chosen "home sites."

Runquist seems to have addressed all these factors with his system for finding and working over shallow-water fish. His hotspots are high in oxygen, bait is plentiful and walleyes feed there often. Moreover, his unique presentation triggers fish by appealing to their senses of sight, taste and texture. In other words, Runquist fishes shallow feeding grounds and tips his jigs with fresh minnow heads that he "jiggles."

Jiggling 101

When we talk about "jiggling," we're not talking about jigging strokes that winter anglers customarily use. Nobody works a jig quite like Runquist. While most anglers perform a lift-and-drop method that varies from twitching to hopping, or from dancing to pumping, Runquist uses one basic jigging stroke all year long. And it works.

True jiggling is a subdued rodtip movement that's difficult to describe, yet relatively easy to master. (Once you get the hang of it you won't forget.) Rather than doing an up-and-down jigstroke, let your entire forearm, not just your wrist, vibrate back and forth at a 45-degree angle. Runquist may use an occasional double rod-pump to call distant fish in, but the jiggling motion is what gets them to bite.

It's easy to tell if your jiggling meets the Runquist standard. If you look at your bait in the ice hole, only the treble hook should rock back and forth; the ice jig's main body should remain relatively stable. If the jig dances at all, you're giving the bait too much motion. Cut back. But if the minnow head on the treble hook isn't swinging back and forth constantly, you must increase the tempo.

Runquist has learned over the years that not all baits can be jiggled effectively. His current favorite is Northland's minnow-shaped Fire-Eye. He also likes Kastmasters, Pimples and Rocker Minnows. Each share a common thread: a slender body and a treble hook on a split-ring. The split-ring is necessary for allowing the minnow head to rock. Incidentally, treble hooks seem to stick more fish than single hooks.

The key is getting the minnow head (a perch eye also works, but check local regulations) to rock or quiver from side to side. If your jig has too much built-in action, it competes with the minnow head. There are exceptions. For example, last winter I experienced some success jiggling a ¼-ounce Cicada, a popular blade bait on Lake Erie.

Another secret to effective jiggling is resisting the temptation to halt the bait when a fish suddenly appears. "You don't stop a bait when a muskie or bass follows," Runquist says. "Why stop for a fish under the ice? It'll usually spook. Maintain the steady action and you'll catch most of the fish that you see."

Through The Looking Glass

See fish? Yep, with Runquist's technique, you'll be fishing water so shallow you can usually see the fish before the hit. The real beauty of the system is knowing if fish are present but not active. You can't know in deep water even with electronics, but you sure can in shallow water! In frigid weather, peer below from inside a portable ice tent; during balmy days, lay on the ice and drape a jacket over your head. "Fish watching" is addictive. You'll get a cram course on winter fish behavior from a single outing! Walleyes aren't the only species you'll see on the flats. Tullibees, perch, burbot, pike and bass also work the shallows in winter. Each behaves differently. For example, if a sleek silvery shadow seems to do a figure eight around your jig several times before hitting, it's a tullibee. Perch, on the other hand, seem to dart in, shove on the brakes, and either smack the bait or dart away.

Walleyes are less predictable. Sometimes they'll slam the bait in a golden blur, and sometimes they gently mouth it. Quite often your line won't move an inch, yet the jig has disappeared. If this is the case, set the hook! Just as likely, a fish will swim through exhibiting a number of body languages. The "rub snub" is a classic: A fish gently rubs its side on the bait as it slowly glides beneath the ice hole. Of course, walleyes often scoot in from nowhere. They might annihilate the jig—brace yourself. But just as often they mysteriously lose interest and glide out of sight.

"There's never a dull moment, even when walleyes aren't hitting," says Runquist. "You get an appreciation for each species, too. They're all different, all fascinating in their own way."

Indeed. A crayfish darts out from a clump of moss and clicks its claws defiantly at your jig. Suddenly, the lake floor moves; it's a mottled burbot. Perch in a myriad of sizes and color patterns swim curiously by. Tullibees inscribe their "infinity" signatures below. Ah, the shallow zone. A world of underwater entertainment awaiting your discovery.

Shallow-Water Structure

Not all structure attracts walleyes on an equal basis. The shal-

Perch are a bonus of fishing the shallow flats as this angler has discovered. In most cases, the angler can see the fish before it hits.

low zone is no exception. Runquist prefers two main types: flats and bars. Both offer a more consistent bite than traditional points, rock piles and weedbeds. What's more, flats and bars continue to produce late in the season when most ice anglers have given up.

Better yet, if you're looking for some untapped water, check out key flats and bars on nearby lakes. Chances are you'll have them all to yourself. "I believe every lake supports active schools of walleyes in the shallows," Runquist says. "The fish graze like sheep along these shallow food shelves. If anglers learn what to look for, they'll be in for a treat."

The most productive shallow zone varies from lake to lake. Generally, the 5- to 9-foot layer is hottest, but fish can be as deep as 12 feet. Short-stemmed cabbage beds (no taller than a foot) and water clarity affect the fish zone in many lakes. As a rule, the more weeds, the clearer the water and the deeper the fish are likely to be found.

Also, fish typically run deeper earlier in the year. But as ice thickens, they gradually creep shallower—shallower than anglers are accustomed to fishing. In fact, in late winter it's common to set the hook and yank the fish out of the hole in one motion!

Most of Runquist's "spots" range from 100 yards to a half mile long. "The fish could be anywhere," he says. "Many days I've drilled 150 to 200 holes. Walleyes in shallow water don't seem to stick around for more than a couple of days. They're pretty nomadic fish."

All of his favorite flats share a common trait: sand bottoms with scattered moss. This sounds heretical as far as winter walleye structure goes, but the combination has paid off for Runquist for the past 20 years. "I may learn a few new spots each year," he says, "but the fish seem to stick to the same general areas year after year. One bar or flat may be hotter than the others, but over the long run they'll all produce."

Scattered fish means you need shortcuts. First, follow the seasonal pattern. During the early ice period, work the edges of the steepest breaks and look for cabbage. During mid-season, fish a bit shallower and work the sides and tops (most cabbage has died off). For late ice, concentrate on the top (especially the dishes) of extensive flats.

And don't forget the daily fish pattern: Fish deeper during midday, and ease to shallow in late afternoon.

It may be a nice walleye—perhaps the largest you've taken—but it may be only a "grazer." Runquist suggests that you not spend a lot of time waiting for another one like it. Move to a more productive spot.

Because these fish are "grazers," forget ambushing at a "spot on the spot." Instead, keep moving until you find them. "And be ready to move some more to stay with the pack," warns Runquist. "Don't spend more than 10 to 15 minutes at any location if you don't see action right away. If the action dies after a burst of activity, I reach for the power auger."

The best way to zero in on the fish is to cut a series of holes along the bar or flat with a power auger. Be sure to cover the top, each end and both sides, regardless of size. Four anglers working together as a team are ideal for large flats and bars; two or three anglers are enough for areas under 200 yards.

When you finally find the fish, circle the hole that produces the first fish, and expect a lot of action. The fish are in a shallow zone for a simple reason: to eat.

A Jiggler's Rig

Jiggling isn't the most demanding of presentations, but some special equipment sure makes the job easier.

Take rods, for example. In shallow water, Runquist prefers short, stout graphite rods. Longer rods work in deeper water, where a longer rod sweep reduces line stretch and displaces the fish. But in shallow water, they "get in the way," says Runquist.

"Pick a 36- to 42-inch rod with a solid butt section and a little give at the tip. Thorne Brothers, Mitchell and Berkley all make good rods, but you have to inspect them closely."

Reels take a pounding. Heavy-duty models with a smooth drag are a must. Runquist advocates duct-taping the reel to the rod for optimum feel and comfort. Daiwa's SS 700 is a good winter reel. Eight-pound-test line (Runquist fishes either Stren or Trilene XT, not XL) is a good choice for most jiggling applications.

Color preferences for fish seem to vary from lake to lake and week to week. Fire orange, hot pink or blue/glow Fire-Eye Minnows, Gold Kastmasters and two-tone green Pimples and Rockers top the list.

14

Western Walleye Fever

by Steve Payne

Droning hypnotically, the thin cables slice through the strong current. Trolling rodtips tremble with responsive lure action below, and far to the side the occasional surge of planer board resistance to the flowage is evident. One rod dips low, hesitates briefly, then springs dramatically skyward, "alive with action." A dedicated hookset, and all hands tense as 8-pound line peels easily. Angler Bob Knopf cautiously adjusts the drag, and in short order, works a chunky, 9-pound walleye to the net.

Before this beautiful creature can be released, two other rods signal identical situations. Thus, with two downrigger cables below and a pair of aggressive river walleyes on lightweight tackle, activity levels escalate until both fish are carefully netted and returned to the river. Amazingly, during the course of two days on the river, rarely do we boat a walleye under 5 pounds. And all this is taking place in the Pacific Northwest, where steelhead, cutthroat and king salmon reign.

Ironically, walleyes have been the prime species sought across much of America east of the Rockies. Virtually thousands of lakes and rivers east of the Continental Divide and across several Canadian provinces have long been the vacation target for many Western fishermen seeking an opportunity to fish for walleyes— but not anymore! That theory is losing credence because the walleye assumes an "active" role in Western waters, as well.

In the Pacific Northwest, where trout and salmon have main-

Ed Iman who has become a master guide on the Columbia River shows off a walleye which is his personal best. It weighed just a few ounces short of 18 pounds.

Western Walleye Fever

tained top billing, a series of vast, sprawling reservoirs and big rivers have come to be recognized as some of the finest walleye fishing opportunities anywhere. Tales of trophy-class fish are true in most cases, but giant salmon and steelhead fresh from the salt are the foremost targets of Western anglers. And that generally leaves walleye fishermen very lonely.

Head West, Pardners

To experience this dynamic, untapped resource, then, plan now. Assemble an assortment of the most effective tackle, a few rods and a big net. Toss in your raingear, longjohns and a cowboy hat. Head way out West. You've arrived when you see sandy prairies, massive volcanic rock outcroppings, raging whitewater and the merging of many small rivers into one gigantic river, the Columbia, home of some of the largest walleyes in the country.

It's here where upstream summer winds churn the current into a rage of seething frenzy, mixing the brown clay of the crudely rugged shoreline with the flowage developed from scores of lesser rivers and streams, and where much of the high-country runoff water west of the Rockies blends to form a churning maze of chocolate-covered whitecaps.

On the Columbia, thriving throughout most of the river system, walleyes grow in this forage-rich environment to phenomenal proportions. And there are lots of them. Where the river forms the boundary between Oregon and Washington, a walleye isn't big until it's 15 pounds! Ten-pound fish are abundant, 12-pounders are common and 14-pounders happen all too frequently. The current Oregon record stands at a mere ¼-ounce under 20 pounds; Washington's exceeds 18 pounds. Even in Idaho where gigantic steelhead, world-class rainbows and record-breaking bull elk command respect, walleyes in that size/weight range have made a limited impression on native sportsmen. In fact, many fish approaching such monstrous proportions never even touch a scale. But Western walleye anglers, although few in number, have learned that the species is superb tablefare as well as abundantly available.

Columbia River Breakthrough

The Columbia River is only a small part of the overall walleye range in the West. A dozen enormous reservoirs grow big walleyes

Feeder streams from the mountains carry heavy loads of food nutrients and oxygen that attract baitfish and, of course, the big walleyes that feed on these baitfish.

in ideal conditions with practically unlimited forage. In Washington—the leading area within the Western walleye range—major reservoirs created by U.S. Corps Of Engineers dam projects including Roosevelt, Banks, the Potholes, Soda, Billy Clapp and a host of additional mammoth walleye waters are scattered across the state's river corridor. All of them are effortlessly producing "easy" sizes for locals who fish them.

The big river, though, contains a variety of fish-holding structure. Coarse, rocky slopes range from shallow shelf-like benches to depths reaching 140 to 190 feet. Huge underwater mountains—some reaching almost to the water's surface, often connected by submerged saddles, or ridges and scores of islands, back bays and massive gravel bars—pose a hazard for some anglers. Current breaks created by protruding points, well-defined (but extremely crude) structure and untold numbers of side streams all hold fish, as do backwater "slicks" below dams. Most side streams and inflows entering either the numerous reservoirs or larger rivers flow heavily laden with food nutrients and oxygen from high mountain elevations or long distances through rugged food-gathering canyons with towering volcanic rock walls.

Prime forage for Western walleyes includes "slow" trout fingerlings. Walleyes are simply not in the same speed league as rainbows, cutthroats or salmon; however, because of the devastating effects of hydroelectric dams, many fish are injured or killed in the turbines. Therefore, prime walleye fishing is often directly downstream from the discharge where larger fish congregate to forage on easy prey. Also, juvenile salmon, crayfish, smelt, a burgeoning population of whitefish and other bottom-dwelling creatures serve to help big walleyes grow bigger. The main forage, however, is yellow perch and small squawfish, a Western trash species.

Early Rising Western Walleyes

As early as late February, fish begin their deep-water staging prior to the start of the spawn. They're found on the steep, breaking edges of shoreline flats or submerged reefs as much as 30 to 60 feet deep but away from current flow. Spawning areas include sand/gravelly mouths of side streams, broad gravel bars on the river's outer bends, long, tapering slopes of hundreds of islands or connecting underwater ridges.

Spawning periods are closed to angling in some Washington waters, but the river is open year-round. A brief recuperative time follows, then fishing becomes red hot! But, not for everyone. Because of the ever-changing bottom structure, the fluctuating water levels and varying depths coupled with clear water/brown water and currents which change almost hourly, certain catching techniques are more successful than others.

Learning The River

Thus, an angler who specializes in conventional leadhead jig fishing will score some fish, as will the shore caster, the spinner and crawler angler, crankbait trollers and walleye hunters who use several tactics. The most consistently successful walleye anglers in the West, however, are those who learn the deep-water haunts of the brute-class fish, the largest fish in the entire system, and that could involve a lifetime. A lifetime, that is, without the services of the most dynamic walleye guide on the river. Few men—save the select breed who operate the giant tugboats which propel huge barges through the river's varying course—know the river as well as Ed Iman. Actually, Iman learned the river on the tugs. As a youth, he worked aboard these vessels, and spent many long hours gazing at the battery of electronics which helped guide the craft. He learned the river's secrets, its deepest channels, bars, reefs and hidden rock mounds; hence, it became a marriage—his river knowledge and his love for fishing this flowage.

When walleyes began to appear in Indian nets some two decades ago, it immediately piqued his interest. While trolling for 40-pound salmon, he caught an occasional walleye. In short order, he abandoned the salmonids in search of the ever-growing walleyes. With an intimate knowledge of the entire river gained while providing a full-time guiding service, he quickly began to catch walleyes in the double-digit weight range, attracting walleye enthusiasts and professional anglers from across the country. He was invited to join the professional staffs of many fishing product manufacturers, and restructured his guiding activities to concentrate on walleyes.

Iman's personal best fish is a trophy-class specimen just 4 ounces short of 18 pounds. Admittedly, he's pledged to release such specimens, but has indeed seen many larger. "The largest walleye I've seen here?" he says. "A gorgeous 23-pound-plus fish caught in an Indian gill net. It was incredible! I weighed it on a scale in my boat, and that was after it had time to dehydrate somewhat. No question, there are even larger fish in this system, though. We've seen them, my clients have hooked them and I fully expect the new-world-record walleye will come from the mid-Columbia."

Secrets Of A River Guide

Iman knows the river. "Following spawning," he says, "big walleyes roam broad gravel bars in 12 to 30 feet of water. Generally, current is slow around spawning time. In the gravel bar areas, which are mostly far downstream from dam sites, the river is wide with miles of rugged structure. Here, we like to troll crawlers on snelled harness rigs with spinner blades. Bottom-dragging weights hold lures in the fish-catching zone, and most folks use types with

Downriggers And Planer Boards For Walleye

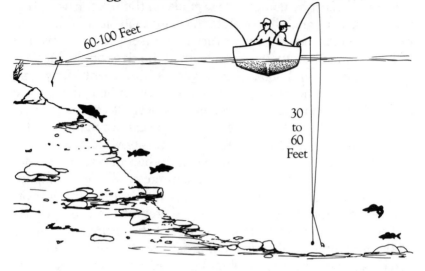

A combination of downriggers and planer boards is highly successful in catching big walleyes. The downrigger handles the deep water and the planer board works the shallower water along the breakline.

protruding wire legs in order to eliminate 'hanging up' on the rocky bottom.

"Trollers catch big fish with deep-diving, minnow-type lures on leaded line, or with three-way swivel/weight setups a couple feet ahead of the lure on mono line. Sometimes, to avoid snagging bottom, I tie a floating minnow-type lure to a 3-foot piece of mono line. This is then fastened to the upper leg of a large safety pin-style, rock-crawler weight. This rig maintains good bottom contact and doesn't hang up."

In the West, the most interesting method for catching big walleyes in deep water involves the use of downriggers. They do the job efficiently with lightweight line, putting the bait directly on the river bottom—where the fish are. Iman mounts a pair of downriggers on a specially designed platform across the transom of his 20-foot boat. He places as many as four, long-handled trolling rods equipped with baitcasting reels in the rod holders.

"Good drag systems are the key," Iman says. "That and lightweight line. I run a straight forward 10-pound test. No fancy stuff. Some guys like to troll a floating minnow-type lure attached as much as 50 or more feet behind a downrigger weight. Not me. I like to shorten up to about 8 feet, 10 at the most. The bottom's rough, all rock in most areas. That much line out costs lures and fishing time."

Trolling speed is no faster than necessary to activate the lure, and anglers troll downstream in slow-flow times, or simply hold position when the current is fast.

To watch Iman control boat position, speed and rodtip response, while constantly monitoring bottom-sensing locators on his boat is simply captivating. A sonar unit which scans forward or to each side of the boat will pick up fish as much as 100 feet away. Also, to keep the lure at the correct depth, he continually monitors the downrigger cable for any drag or resistance. At the first indication of a weight bumping bottom, he just touches a control button, or cranks the handle once or twice raising or lowering the weight/lure setup.

Included among the hottest jigging lures used on the Columbia River are the Jim-E-Jig (top) and the Jim-E-Spin. Products of Triple "J" Lures, these lures are particularly effective when worked through stream mouths.

Get The Lead Down

Leadhead jigs account for fish in calm water at various depths. The lighter weights work well in slow water, but often fishing in strong, 3- to 5-knot current requires lures in the ⅜-ounce range or more to maintain bottom contact. Tube jigs are regular producers, but leadheads that develop some form of action are even better.

Some companies produce jigs with spinner blades that flash and attract fish as the lure is gently raised and lowered in slow current. Some are scent/salt treated and come in vibrant colors. The technique is easy, and Ed Iman is a master at fishing jigs.

"First, I like to locate a particular underwater reef or hump, which may be as much as a mile long," he says. "One I know has been a producer recently. By drifting with the current along the drop-off edges, we pick up walleyes; however, most are always on the reef's edges. It's easy to teach my clients to give a simple lift-and-lower action to the lure. At 50 feet, though, strikes are not strikes or even solid weight. They're just a different sensation. A feeling you sort of develop, kinda like pulling a lure from a honey jar. You just know." Iman's walleye clients quickly adapt to these instructions and respond with powerful hooksets.

Also, they're instructed that it's important to maintain a tight line but also to reel in the fish very slowly so that it can be released safely.

Walleye Lights And Spoons

Some special lures have carved a deep niche for themselves in Western walleye anglers' tackle arsenals. Jigging spoons especially are "hot" in deep water. The legalizing of glow-in-the-dark and battery-operated, lighted lures have created new vistas for deep-water walleye fishing in the West.

These lures have been super fish-catchers for many years, of course. With the added touch of "glow," they're dynamite, especially during low-light periods, in stained water or following a heavy rain. Trollers in the West have traversed deep, underwater haunts for walleyes, using spinners, plugs, jigs—the works—only to retrace their path with a hammering, bottom-bumping jigging spoon for taking easy limits.

These exciting salmon lures account for great walleyes anytime, but are superb in the dark. Generally, in-the-know anglers

Here is one of Iman's obviously satisfied customers holding a good-sized Columbia River walleye taken while trolling at dusk. Low-light situations usually mean better walleye fishing.

attach a short trailer hook and "sweeten" the spoon with a piece of nightcrawler or perch meat. A small swivel attached to the spoon prevents line twisting. Most spoon jiggers prefer lures weighing ½ ounce or more, which makes for a good "feel." Best colorations include luminous tint on one side, with an orange, yellow, chartreuse or green on the reverse side. Also, hammered gold, chrome or metallic shades are good. Most anglers use a crawler, or pork rind on the hook point and extended to the rear trailer.

Iman often "holds" the boat in strong current at an inflowing stream's mouth or slightly upstream of a hump, hole or underwater ridge. It's a simple matter of casting cross-current into the fish-holding zone and then allowing the lure to settle on the bottom. Lifting the rodtip only slightly allows the current to carry it to the "slick" water at the flow's edges. "It's the edges that'll hold the fish," Iman says, "and it's where the lure will be most effective." Slightly hopping a jig or spoon lets the current carry it to the walleyes. In time, the current moves the lure into "dead" water. At this time, lower the rodtip and reel in the lure quickly to avoid hang-ups; then repeat. Two casters can easily cover acres of water this way. Some anglers tip the lure with a tiny piece of flannel cloth or sponge dipped in a favorite attractant scent. "I prefer crawlers or a small piece of fish," Iman says.

By The Light Of The Moon

There are times when Ed Iman wouldn't consider a bright, sunny day on the water. Time spent on the river, and a keen sense of walleye behavioral patterns subtly dictate the times when walleye angling might be fruitless. Iman and a scarce breed of walleye addicts have learned the advantages of nightfishing on large reservoirs. These anglers have studied walleye habits and quickly adapted to nightfishing. Again, trolling is the preferred method, and the outer edge of huge, weed-covered flats is the hotspot. Water may range from 12 to 20 feet along the deepest edges; however, experience shows that the fish will generally be shallower. Nighttime tactics involve using big lures, such as big minnow-imitator types; bulky, plastic-jig dressings; and oversized spinner blades and rattling plugs.

Nightfishing also demands quiet. Hushed electric trolling motors, long lines and "S"-style trolling patterns across enormous flats produce good results. Strong vibrating lures have become popular with Western steelhead/salmon anglers, and so it follows that they would be equally enjoyed by walleye fishermen. Especially attractive are those lures designed to bump bottom, stir up mud or create activity.

"As for colors, I think most night guys like the chromes," says Iman, "but I go with chartreuse, hot tiger, yellow/orange or white. Also, I tie a short piece of heavier line to a small snap swivel and then to the main line. The bottom is where night fish will be, and heavier line doesn't fray as easy on the gravel and sand.

"A neat, well-organized boat, free of excess gear and other noisy hazards is important for nightfishing," Iman continues. "I've seen $100 rods broken, tackle boxes destroyed and worse. Some guys lay out a string of glowing floats as marker lines, others simply wait for moonlight. You do whatever it takes at night, and the fishing can be the best ever.

"Nighttime trolling speed is critical," he says. "Slow speeds are best. Fish are quick to overtake a well-presented lure, and faster-than-necessary trolling usually results in lost time." When trolling upstream, some anglers move the boat in a wide zig-zag pattern cross-current, covering maximum fish-holding flats. The best nighttime efforts result from spending a day or two just learning various landmarks, direction and current patterns. Still, it all becomes different after dark.

Trout And Salmon

15

Taming The Great Lakes Currents

by Tom Huggler

urrent is something the better trollers understand; they know how to fish it to their advantage. For example, they know where fish lie in relation to current and how nomadic species like salmon and some trout use it for travel purposes as well as for feeding and comfort zones. The most skillful anglers are intimate with current problems, including tricky flows beneath the surface. They know how to make effective lure and bait presentations regardless of current velocity.

In any of the five Great Lakes, current must be handled properly because it will make or break a salmon troller's game plan. And that's the truth.

Current comes from many sources. The 5,747 Great Lakes tributaries delivering flows ranging from mere trickles to raging torrents have much to do with this phenomenon. Combined, the Great Lakes contain 95,000 surface acres of water, about 20 percent of the planet's freshwater supply. Powerful winds with their miles of fetch can raise the level of these watery pastures to 8 feet on the opposite shore. Also creating currents are bottom structure, condensation and evaporation, the spring-summer rollover of cold water to warm water, and lunar tides. Even on the most placid days, unseen currents contribute to fishing dynamics.

Nowhere is this more true than in Lake Ontario, presently a trolling hotspot for big salmon. Although the smallest of the five Great Lakes in terms of surface area, Lake Ontario is the second-deepest lake after Superior. Although Ontario is only 193 miles

Captain Bob Cinelli nets a 14-pound king salmon for the author who was able to mix business with pleasure on this trip. The fish hit a Southport Slammer spoon with a great deal of authority.

Taming The Great Lakes Currents

171

long and 53 miles wide, its average depth is nearly 300 feet. The large volume of mostly cold water provides outstanding salmon fishing while contributing to enormous temperature fluctuations which cause—and in turn are caused by—current. Because of the lake's east-to-west orientation, prevailing westerlies are allowed a clean sweep, but the biggest factor that contributes to current dynamics is the inflow from the Niagara River.

The mighty Niagara is more like a strait than a river. According to engineers at New York Power Authority, which operates a river dam, the Niagara sends about 1½ million gallons of water each second, on the average, into the southwestern end of Lake Ontario. Besides pumping food into the lake, the Niagara's emerald-gray plume travels the lake's entire length, creating temperature and color edges for zooplankton, baitfish, trout and salmon.

How powerful is this current? "Olcott, New York, lies 18 miles east of the river's outflow," says Bob Cinelli, one of Lake Ontario's most respected charter-boat captains. "A mile off shore from the harbor village is a 5-foot-high buoy. I have seen currents moving so fast through this area that they literally bury the buoy some distance underwater."

I fished with Cinelli for the first time in 1987 when he was a 28-year-old skipper already building a reputation for knowing where to find fish and how to catch them. "Probably 90 percent of the lake is unused at any given time," he says. "Trout and salmon may travel through some of that large volume of water, but the truth is they hold and feed in only 10 percent of it. Those are the fish I look for, and current is the place I begin my homework."

In spring, the Niagara River is a blessing because it freights food and is warmer than the surrounding lake. Salmon and trout flock to it. Shallow Lake Erie warms faster than deeper Lake Ontario, and the Niagara River is the conduit for the tepid flow. A northwest wind loads the southern Lake Ontario shoreline with warm water, and trollers begin scoring in the Niagara County shallows off Fort Niagara State Park, Wilson, Olcott and Golden Hill State Park. Fishing also picks up in Orleans and Monroe counties, all the way to Rochester.

Later in summer and into fall, activity at ports east of Rochester turn on. Sodus Bay is good. So are Oswego and the Salmon River at Pulaski. From east to west, these are the locations that

Cinelli sets up his trolling spread. Note how close the downriggers are to the boat's corners. "Corner out-downs outproduce all other locations," Cinelli says emphatically.

Taming The Great Lakes Currents

typically receive from 100,000 to 600,000 spring fingerling chinooks raised in hatcheries each year.

Cinelli unwraps his boat each April and trolls close to shore, where his ice-out bag is typically mixed with cohos, browns, rainbows, kings and a few lake trout. By early May, he motors out a mile beyond the 70-foot mark. There, through August, he runs a spoon program for kings. That is unusual because most other fishermen mix spoons with plugs, and some run purely a plug program. "Spoons just work better for me," Cinelli says.

Colors are important to Cinelli's success. The hot color in early morning is typically chartreuse; however, as the day brightens, the skipper mixes in black, then switches over to pink by afternoon. As the sun works its way toward the western horizon, he gradually merges in blacks again. By nightfall, his metal spread is solid black.

The first time I fished with him, I immediately noticed that Cinelli had mounted all four of his downriggers close to the boat corners. I wondered why.

"The reason is simple," he says. "Corner out-downs outproduce all other locations." And with that he sent down a pair of Yeck Spoons to 50 and 55 feet and then stacked them with similar lures at 5 and 10 feet above. He then clipped Southport Slammers (locally called Cyclops spoons) to the transom-mounted downriggers and sent them down to 40 and 45 feet. Bob's trolling pattern is, therefore, a slightly inverted V with lead lengths all kept short at 5 to 10 feet for better hooksetting.

We were stitching the color seam where the darker Niagara River flow merged with the bright blue of Lake Ontario in 70 feet of water off Olcott. The wind began to cry through the downrigger wires, and I watched the cocked rods lean ahead and ease back like racehorses at the starting gate. I felt tremendous anticipation, a sixth sense that I often experience when trolling the big lakes. I just knew that things were about to bust loose.

Suddenly, a doubled-over rod flashed upward like a sprung switchblade. I had it in my hands before Cinelli could holler, "Fish on!" The salmon streaked up and away, like big kings always do, stripping off about 100 feet of line before cracking the surface. When he rolled, the sun caught and reflected on his silver side. Then he sounded. Ten minutes later, I muscled him into the net. My first Lake Ontario king was no monster at almost 14 pounds. It was, however, a fine, healthy gamefish with iridescent flanks that gleamed like a purple oil slick.

"Toss him back," Cinelli said.

"Toss him back?" I replied.

"Yeah. He's under 15 pounds. We'll get bigger fish," he said. And we did.

The Niagara River water moves quickly from west to east, requiring only about six hours for current from the river mouth to reach Olcott. When the flow hits 30 Mile Point (about 12 miles farther east), it turns northeast and gushes into the lake, then falls south again on its way to Oak Orchard. By now, it usually has mixed with colder lake water, resulting in a better summer salmon fishery at Oak Orchard than at Olcott. South or southwest winds are favored now because they push warm water to Canada. Northwest winds in particular are bad news because they bring warm water in close to shore. During one recent summer, fishing was poor because the water was 72 degrees from the surface to 120 feet deep. The near-shore waters became a desert with fish abandoning the area for colder climates. The next summer, however, southerly winds prevailed, and angling success improved dramatically. But current makes the lake schizophrenic, and its mood changes are hard to predict.

"It would amaze you what can happen out there in such a short period of time," Cinelli says. "A typical scenario in late June will have a northeast wind blowing hard for two days, changing the top-to-bottom water column from warm to cold (sometimes 39 to 41 degrees) and stacking it along the western shore. Suddenly the wind stops and switches to the southwest. Within mere hours the surface temperature will rise to 70 degrees, a temperature band will develop in the middle, and the lake basement will become 39 degrees. You have to understand this kind of phenomenon if you're going to fish this lake with any success."

Throughout the Great Lakes, current dynamics begin in early spring when offshore breezes turn over water, forcing the colder, denser layer (the hypolimnion) deep and heating the upper level (the epilimnion). Underwater currents are created and further influenced by structure, pounding waves and tributary discharges. These dynamics cause warm-water patches to occur at various places, usually close to shore. Good spots to troll besides the color line include the upper layer of sun-warmed shallows, wave troughs

Finding Thermal Bar Edge In Great Lakes

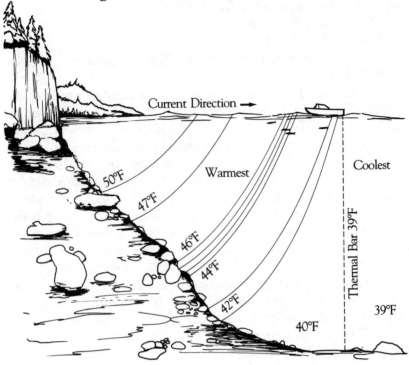

Current Direction →

50°F

47°F

46°F

44°F

42°F

40°F

Warmest

Coolest

Thermal Bar 39°F

39°F

A thermal bar is a springtime phenomenon resulting from warmer water advancing into the lake's deeper, colder water. Trout and salmon love it and are found along temperature breaks.

that parallel shore and sandwich sandbars to either side and thermal discharges from factories and power plants.

Another current and warm water source is the thermal bar, which is created when a lake turns over each spring. Here is what happens: Freshwater becomes densest at 39 degrees during winter. As portions of the Great Lakes freeze at 32 degrees, this 39-degree water sinks to the bottom. As we have seen, spring runoff and the sun's rays combine to warm the upper layer, forcing the lower layer deeper. When inshore water temperatures are less than 39 degrees, a vertical wall of water called an "interface" or "thermal bar" results.

Fish love it.

This thermal bar moves slowly offshore until sometime in late spring or summer when rollover is complete and the summer thermocline (a more-or-less horizontal water band where the epilimnion and hypolimnion mix) forms. The thermal bars are another temperature break. Cinelli and other savvy fishermen monitor them with surface temperature probes.

Slicks, identified by smooth water surrounded by ripples, are excellent clues to a thermal bar which could be a hundred yards to one-half mile across. Sometimes a riptide is created; other times the edge is fog-shrouded. Slicks can occur at any time during the long trolling season, and the wise angler keeps an eye out for them.

"Dead-flat days are the best," Cinelli claims, "because I can see what's going on. River highways develop on the surface with oil-type slicks next to chops. Sometimes the color actually changes, and sometimes we notice trash lines developing. These are windrowed lines of leaves, duck weed and other debris, even pollen. Such current and temperature edges are what both baitfish and trout and salmon seek."

In summer, Cinelli avoids the Niagara River plume because it is typically too warm to attract fish. That's when he focuses on other currents and temperature breaks. Many trollers switch over to lake trout by June or July when both trout and salmon are apt to be in 200 to 300 feet of water, which is about two to three miles from shore. Salmon are more difficult to catch in summer because they wander more than lakers. Finding the elusive kings can be a tough hunting game. Cinelli sticks with kings because he usually can find them, and they are more exciting to catch. He uses his electronics, including a Lowrance LMS 300 liquid-crystal sonar unit equipped with Loran C and plotter, to find currents and to move with the fish.

"Three sets of numbers from electronics on my boat tell me how much current I am dealing with and which direction it is coming from," he says. "The first number is my surface speed indicator (the LMS 300, which also measures temperature). The second is a speed indicator (fishhawk Monitroll) at the down-rigger weight. The third measures boat speed over the lake bottom (a loran unit reading)."

Any veteran Great Lakes troller will admit that maintaining the correct trolling speed is the most critical of many variables for success. Because of surface flows, winds and tricky underwater currents, a boat could be moving 6 mph while the lures are hang-

Inverted V-shaped Rigging Pattern

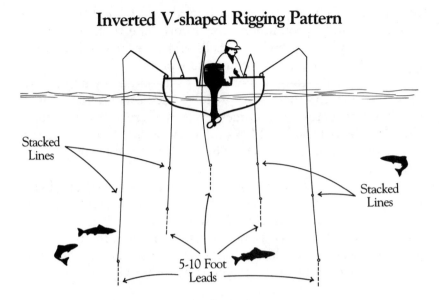

Cinelli uses an inverted V-shaped rigging pattern in trying to completely cover the water that he is trolling. In addition to running downriggers at differing depths, he also "stacks" lures.

ing dead in the water. Cinelli factors in the information from his electronics to maintain a steady 2- to 2.5-mph troll. He does this most easily by trolling downcurrent with the wind direction. Going with the flow also helps him to cover more water quickly and to cut the amount of time needed to turn a hunting game into a catching one.

Figure eights and S-turns help present lures in interesting ways, triggering strikes from trailing salmon. That's why Cinelli angles his lures into available current, even to the point of crossing the current at right angles. His theory is that salmon at rest usually face into the current, although he also knows they will chase a lure that imitates a crippled baitfish. The only problem current poses is how it can hamper lure presentation. That is why Cinelli works so hard to both quantify and qualify any flow he encounters.

"Another point to remember is that no boat trolls straight," Cinelli says, "unless it is equipped with twin screws (propellers) that are balanced. A single prop pulls the boat one way or the other. If the driver doesn't work the steering wheel and angle his lures into the current, the boat will crab out." Cinelli also believes that because every boat handles differently, anglers need to spend a lot of time trolling with experimental lure spreads. The inverted V mentioned earlier is the pattern that works best for him because his lures remain relatively free of tangles.

Lake Ontario salmon action peaks in mid-September when the brawling spawners, including fish weighing more than 40 pounds, move into natal-release areas. In early to mid-August, Cinelli breaks out dodgers and flies, especially after he has located fish. He usually stacks the big metal attractors with spoons; but he sometimes runs a small diving crankbait five feet above the attractor. Leads usually are tight (5 to 10 feet).

Hands down, however, spoons take 80 percent of the 1,500 trout and salmon brought aboard his boat each year. Many are released to fight again. Why spoons?

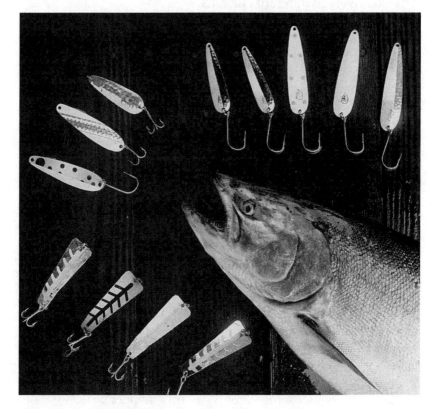

These spoons, which are all successful spoons for salmon, have one important point in common. The slim shape of these spoons improve the spoons' capacity for solid hooksets because salmon have small mouths.

"Well, I'm certainly more confident using them," Cinelli admits, "but the truth is spoons give me a better hookup percentage. Because we troll, these fish have to hook themselves. Thin, flat spoons fit into their mouths better. The round shape of most plugs give a hooked fish more leverage to throw the steel." The search for the best possible hookset methods also prompts the savvy skipper to file hooks to pinprick sharpness and to screw down his short releases as tightly as possible.

Because they are rubber-bodied and flexible, squid also provide solid hooksets; sometimes Cinelli runs them in early summer. Their drawback is that they must be mated to attractors, which slows the hunting game considerably. Cinelli has more than 5,000 spoons aboard his charter boat but relies on four major brands to cover the spectrum of trolling speeds, from .5 to 5 mph, and to fish effectively in different currents.

Pirate spoons are bendable and thin and work best at speeds from 1 to 1.5 mph. They produce when fish are lethargic and currents are minimal. Yeck Spoons don't kick well at slower speeds and are most effective from 2.5 to 5.0 mph. Arrowhead spoons flash and dart from side to side because they are heavier. Cinelli likes them because they impart a different action and are heavy enough to maintain presentation in strong current. Northern King spoons are the most tolerant of speed ranges and can usually be mixed with other brands.

Cinelli buys mostly blank spoons and then doctors them with tape patterns. He likens the process to a stream trout fisherman who enjoys tying his own flies. "Some store-bought patterns work well," he says, "but I have better success when I make little changes such as widening or narrowing stripes and adding eyes."

Top-notch equipment helps the skipper to be consistent. (Cinelli spends about $10,000 annually on gear.) He likes clear, 20-pound-test premium monofilament but admits that the stronger line helps customer-proof his tackle used by neophyte anglers who don't know how to handle salmon. In the hands of an experienced fisherman, 10- to 14-pound-test monofilament will be sufficient.

Keeping gear in good condition and working current to his advantage are obvious ingredients to this skipper's success. But Cinelli watches the little things, too. For example, the size of baitfish that salmon and trout are eating (open bellies occasionally for matching lure size to forage size) is important, as well as how they are taking lures. Aggressive fish usually are hooked in the corner of the mouth. Trailing salmon that just open their mouths and gently suck in food often are hooked in the upper jaw. Switching lures or making presentations at different angles into the current can turn fussy eaters into voracious ones.

"You have to remember that these fish are high-energy eating machines," Cinelli says. "They eat and rest and eat some more. When a salmon wants your lure, he'll come after it like a mad dog. My job is to make him want to take the lure." Indeed. Cinelli figures he needs 30 to 60 hits per day to keep customers happy.

Each of the Great Lakes has its own personality of current and structure and how trout and salmon utilize both. Yet there are similarities. Cinelli's theories on how to fish current effectively were developed over a three-year period when he competed in an annual Lake Michigan tournament off Ludington, Michigan. For years, upwellings and current shears have baffled all but the best trollers. The lessons Cinelli learned at Ludington had immediate application to Lake Ontario and have helped to make him a top skipper instead of just another charter-boat captain.

=======16=======

Fishing A Woolly Bugger

======= by John Holt =======

H aving a rod ripped from one's hands is not an act commonly associated with what is frequently perceived as the genteel pursuit of fly fishing. Long graceful casts and languid floats of tiny, feathered flies that are eventually sipped in by trout displaying the discerning tastes of a Paris gourmet are the accepted vision.

This perception may indeed have some basis in fact, except when the pattern being cast is the Woolly Bugger. This bushy, ugly version of the more sedate woolly worm has taken very large trout throughout the western U.S., on the hallowed limestone streams of Pennsylvania, on the rushing rivers of Patagonia and even on the isolated rivers of Iceland's interior.

While many fly-fishing purists look down their pointed noses at this ungainly fly, serious seekers of big trout know and revere the Woolly Bugger's fish-taking capability. Few serious anglers are found working the water without at least a couple of these things stashed away in their vest somewhere.

There are many theories as to why the Woolly Bugger is so effective: It imitates forage fish, it looks like stone-fly nymphs or it just looks like something big and juicy to eat—something too tempting for a big brown or rainbow or brook trout to pass up.

In Montana where taking big trout is a way of life, any river guide worth his salt fishes a Woolly Bugger sometime during the season, often with his own unique techniques. There are as many ways to effectively fish this pattern as there are skilled fly fishers;

Guide John Adza works the drop-off between a gravel shelf and a deep hole. That's always a prime location for taking big trout that are susceptible to the Woolly-Bugger pattern.

Fishing A Woolly Bugger

however, casual observation by the neophyte reveals that certain basic truths and techniques are manifested by all successful Woolly-Bugger devotees.

John Adza, a western Montana guide and outfitter and the head of Catch Montana, a loose confederation of some of the state's quality guides, is highly skilled at consistently taking big trout and putting his clients onto trophy fish. So it comes as no surprise that he considers Woolly Buggers to be one of the most important weapons in his fly-fishing arsenal.

"Buggers are good anytime of the year," says Adza. "They are the first thing I turn to when the action is not taking place on the surface. Buggers are the 'play at first' in these types of conditions. They are always good for one fish, then I get cute."

Woolly Buggers Come Alive In The Water

One of the prime attributes of this pattern is that the lure seems to come alive in the water. Tied onto a shank hook with a chenille body, bushy marabou feather tail and hackled body, the fly pulses in the water as it drifts in current. Even in an amateur's hands, Woolly Buggers dance and bob over prime lies, looking like a crippled minnow trying to survive a serious malfunction. In the hands of an expert, the fly is deadly. During certain times of the year, notably autumn, a talented angler can take over 100 fish, many of them more than 20 inches long, in a day's float. The strikes are often savage, and frequently more than one trout will rush from bankside cover to attack the lure like a starving pack of wolves.

The fame of the Woolly Bugger is all the more astonishing when one considers that the pattern is of fairly recent vintage. Developed by Russell Blessing in 1967, the fly has become as famous as its much older counterparts such as the Muddler Minnow, Adams and Hare's Ear. Its inventor referred to it as "just another ugly fly" and suggested that it imitates the leeches of his central Pennsylvania limestone streams. Noted angler Barry Beck is generally credited with being the first to bring the pattern to the big, wild waters of the Rockies.

Blessing experimented with various configurations for years before settling on the current design which also looks a bit like a hellgrammite, the larva of the dobsonfly. He had originally intended to trim the hackle short but decided against this when he

While the pattern normally is associated with larger trout, even smaller trout than this brown will take a Woolly Bugger.

noticed the lifelike action of the feathers when he breathed on them. Blessing's daughter named the pattern, and fly-fishing expert Vince Marinaro refers to the tie as "Woolly Boogers." Such is the nature of fame.

Accurate Casting Not Critical

Another virtue of the Woolly Bugger concerns casting. Because of its weight, it is not as easy or pleasurable to work as a small, dry fly, but the very nature of the pattern allows for "sloppy" presentations. The idea is to get the pattern as close to the bank as possible and then begin the retrieve. The best Woolly-Bugger terrain is often undercut and covered with dense brush— ideal habitat for secretive and very large brown trout. Often, an errant or noisy cast actually attracts a trout's attention, the "splat" or "plop" perhaps indicating the presence of a wounded minnow or a large grasshopper. If such a ruckus occurred during a hatch of mayflies, however, every decent trout within a 100-yard radius would race for cover and cease feeding for hours.

"Most of the time I prefer to fish across-stream and then mend (flipping line with the rodtip to eliminate drag from the current and extend the drift or float) downstream in order to swim the bugger," says Adza. "Don't be in a hurry to fish out the cast. Try to get big, long drifts, the kind that present the fly in front of the fish for a long time. Often trout hit the thing at the drift's end as it begins to swing out with the current. You have to be ready at these times because the take is swift and you don't have much line to work with because it is extended by the current's drift.

"A lot of guys strip their line in too fast and zip the bug out of the trout's zone," says Adza. "They're wasting their time when they do this. Big fish often move far out for food moving at a pretty good clip."

This advice seems straight-forward but contradicts 90 percent of the information other anglers give you. Most advise you to whip the Woolly Bugger tight to the bank and then strip it in as fast as possible before making another rocket-like cast and retrieve. Indeed, there are numerous times when this approach is deadly, such as in the fall when browns are on or near their spawning redds and in an extremely aggressive mood. As Adza says, "Buggers are especially good for browns between spawning and cold-weather dormancy." But for most of the year, the trout are not quite so high-strung, so Adza's idea of working the Woolly Bugger in a more methodical way makes good sense.

While most of the discussion so far has centered on the fly's ability to catch brown trout, Woolly Buggers also account for many hefty rainbows, along with good numbers of brook trout and even wild cutthroat trout. Browns tend to be more inclined to eat other fish than are other trout species, but rainbows measured in pounds and not inches are often taken on Woolly Buggers from rivers like the Missouri and Green. The pattern works wherever trout swim.

Weighted Or Unweighted Is The Question
The two basic approaches to tying Woolly Buggers are the weighted and unweighted. Both styles have their proponents.

Adza sets the hook on a brown that nailed a bugger as he retrieved it through a deep run. He carefully plays the fish so that it can be released unharmed.

Those in favor of weight say this helps sink the pattern down to the stream bottom where the bigger fish hang out, while those preferring the lighter models believe their choice has more motion in the water, thereby enticing more trout into striking. Adza likes both points of view.

"When I am working deep runs or pools," he says, "I prefer weighted bugs. They are about the only way to drop down to the fish; however, there are drawbacks. When buggers are fished down deep, they are difficult to control all the way through the drift. The different layers of water and varying currents twist and bend the line creating a good deal of slack.

"A lot of trout are going to take at the drift's end. They chase the bugger all the way downstream and you never know it. You have to do everything possible to keep control of your line, including mending, stripping in slack and just trying to imagine where the bugger is and what it is doing down there," he says.

If this sounds a bit like a psychic conjuring act, in a way it is. Watching master fly fishers does have some of the trappings of observing a wizard creating something from thin air (or in this case, clear water). Concentration and a touch of intuition are vital in this submerged form of angling. Even a vicious hit from a big fish seems muted and subdued through the distance of several feet of water and various current speeds.

As for the unweighted versions, Adza uses them because their increased buoyancy creates a much more "lifelike action" in the water. Adza uses a sink-tip line that has a 10- or even 20-foot, weight-forward section that drops the pattern to the fish. He has found that a weighted line is easier to cast than a weighted bugger, which has a tendency to find the back of the angler's head during the forward movement of the cast, especially during a windy day on the river.

"I keep the tippet (front section of the leader attached to the fly) short and heavy," he says, "maybe 4 to 6 feet for the entire leader and 1X or 2X, 12 pounds, in heavy, murky water. The fish hit hard, and you work through tangles and submerged brush and other debris. You want a tippet that has enough strength to handle these conditions. It's no fun losing buggers on every other cast, and replacing flies can become expensive, too.

"You want something with enough backbone to pick the bug out of the water and to handle strong current and big fish," he continues, "something that is a pleasure to use. If you are under the gun yourself, casting is miserable. Your accuracy suffers tremendously and you won't have much fun. Afterall, that's why you're fishing in the first place."

Brushy Banks Are Prime Turf

Even with a pattern as effective as the Woolly Bugger, you cannot just haul back and fling the contraption out in the middle of the river and expect to hook a trout. The fish have well-defined areas that offer shelter from predators and the current's force. These areas also provide a ready food source.

Undercut, brushy banks are ideal locations. So are drop-offs just behind gravel bars. Logjams and other submerged structure always hold trout. Sometimes deep runs over a broken stream bot-

Working Woolly Buggers Effectively

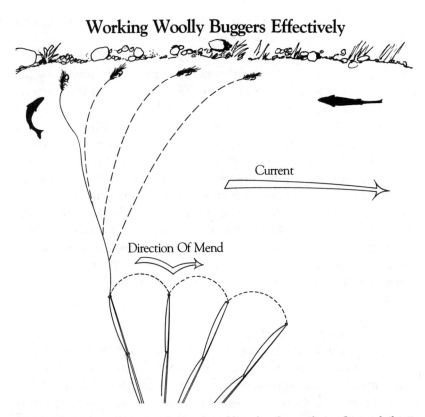

Current

Direction Of Mend

The Woolly-Bugger pattern is cast bank-tight and kept there by mending or flipping the line in small loops downstream, following the drift of the fly. The slack keeps the fly close to the bank.

tom are productive, affording fish plenty of cover. And the current delivers a constant supply of unsuspecting forage fish, like sculpins and minnows, almost directly into the jaws of hungry, waiting trout.

"Most anglers (fishing the bugger) cast to a target area and then strip right in," says Adza. "True, this sometimes produces fish, but allowing the bug to drift and undulate in the current is far more productive. Cast tight to the bank and then roll cast (flip more line with a circular rod motion) toward the bank. Mend line. Do anything needed to get line out to the bug, extending the drift. On good runs downriver, I've drifted a bugger through 100 yards or more of holding water. This is deadly. The fish stack up in the feeding lanes next to the bank and a good drift always means a good fish.

"This takes effort and concentration; however, it is the key to connecting with the really big trout."

The bugger's inventor stated in an article written several years ago that he prefers a "natural downstream drift followed by an across-stream retrieve." Whatever the choice, swim the pattern in as lifelike and enticing manner as possible.

By big fish Adza means over 24 inches. A 20-inch fish is a healthy trout, but once you exceed the 2-foot barrier, you have entered the land of big-time, serious, trophy trout. Hold a 25-inch brown next to a 20-incher and you see the differences. The bigger fish has a much larger, more menacing jaw, a bulging back and is wide and muscular through the shoulders and back. This is the type of fish that buggers are famous for taking. The ones that tear backing from your reel and race downriver like freight trains, sometimes smoking reels and smashing rodtips. A trout like this makes a season and is worth the countless casts and hours of brain-numbing concentration.

Trout Hunting At Its Best

Fishing the banks is best done with unweighted buggers and sink-tip lines. For deep holes and submerged structure, Adza suggests sink-tips and weighted flies. This is difficult fishing, aside from the mental effort involved. Digging line and flying up-and-out of deep, fast-moving water takes work and that 7-weight rod the guide mentioned earlier.

After fishing through the drift, the best way to accomplish the retrieve that begins a new cast is to quickly strip in the line until about 15 or 20 feet remain out in the water. Trout often strike during this frenetic motion, assuming the Woolly Bugger is a minnow fleeing for cover. Also, a 7-weight rod is strong enough to readily pull this amount of line from the stream and create a strong backcast allowing you to shoot the line forward to your next exciting target area.

When you're wading a river, it's easy to locate the next casting target, says Adza. You have all the time in the world to size up the spot. However, when floating in a raft or boat, the angler must not only concentrate on his present cast, but also look ahead and plan his next effort. Practice turns this seemingly difficult routine into almost a habit. As with any of the more productive techniques in angling, practice is the key to success. Most guides spend

Here, the angler has cast to the grassy bank of this stream, and is letting the line drift as it carries the Woolly Bugger along the edge of the stream bank.

Fishing A Woolly Bugger

Working any pattern in a seam between fast and slow water is an excellent way to attract big trout. Allow the fly to dart and then to drift and swim rapidly—anything to draw attention.

100 to 150 days on a given river, so it is easy to see why they outfish most anglers with such consistency.

Selecting The Correct Woolly Bugger

Woolly Buggers are tied in several color combinations ranging from completely olive to bright yellow, and Adza believes the selection should be dictated by water conditions. As a general rule, use olive and olive-and-black combinations when rivers are running clear and at near-normal levels. Brown buggers work as the water begins to go off color. The black tie is perhaps the most productive in cloudy or even muddy water conditions. However, this is only a general guideline and Adza emphasizes that, as with all fly fishing, observation and experimentation are absolutely necessary on any outing.

The most popular combination is a body of olive chenille tied on a 4X-long hook, Nos. 2 to 8, with a black marabou feather tail, black hackle tied along the body length (called palmered) and a black thread head. Lead wire is tied in near the head for weight. Black is another popular color, working particularly well in murky water. Brown with a black tail, hackle and head is also used often.

You may think that a yellow Woolly Bugger is unnatural in most rivers—few prime-trout rivers have indigenous goldfish populations—but there are times (notably in fall) when large brown trout find the color irresistible. This is one color combination that seems to benefit from a cast and then a quick, stripping retrieve.

Adza sometimes likes to tie in a whorl of marabou at the head and a couple of flash-a-bou strands along the body. This material reflects whatever light is available in a river. At times, Woolly Buggers tied with flash-a-bou outfish standard patterns by a substantial margin.

As far as Adza is concerned, the basics of fishing the Woolly Bugger involve drifting the pattern through prime holding areas for as long as possible in a natural manner, matching color combinations to water conditions and selecting either weighted or unweighted buggers depending upon water speed and depth.

While Woolly Buggers do not share the romance and stately fashion of their high-floating brethren, they are, without a doubt, one of the best big-trout producers ever conceived.

17

Lake Trout Through The Ice

by Shawn Perich

W inter in Minnesota's "north country" is either wasteland or wonderland. It depends upon your viewpoint. The snow starts falling in October and is often hip-deep by Christmas. Thirty-below nights are routine. Many days the mercury never rises above zero. In this climate, surfers and sunbathers are out of luck. Ice fishermen, however, couldn't ask for more.

The Canadian Shield, a geological formation, extends across the Minnesota/Ontario border, its presence indicated by a dense boreal forest and myriad, rock-bottomed lakes. This wild country is the bastion of timber wolves and moose. Even woodland caribou have been sighted here. There are few roads, and even fewer dwellings. During the summer, the best way to travel this area is by canoe. In fact, one million acres are included in the Boundary Waters Canoe Area (BWCA), and most of this vast area between the Canadian border and Lake Superior's North Shore, is designated as the Superior National Forest.

Slicing through the conifers is the Gunflint Trail, a serpentine pavement ribbon which extends 60 miles from Grand Marais on the Lake Superior shore to mighty Saganaga Lake on the Canadian border. The Gunflint crosses the Laurentian Divide, which was known as the "Height of Land" to French voyagers who paddled fur-company, freighter canoes through this region two centuries ago. North of the divide, clear waters flow to Hudson Bay; to the south, they spill into Lake Superior.

This angler landed a nice lake trout which was taken on a jig. Snowmobiles can be used on some Gunflint lakes, and are considered an important mode of transportation in these areas.

Lake Trout Through The Ice   195

Changes have occurred beneath these crystalline waters. Oldtimers can remember, often with disgust, when the first pails of wiggling smallmouth bass fingerlings were dumped into lakes so summer resort guests would have some kind of fish to catch when native lake trout were deep. To a simple ecosystem which contained lakers, northern pike, whitefish, burbot and forage species, popular gamefish such as bass, walleyes and brook trout were added. The walleyes and bass found the lakes appealing and spread throughout the interconnected lake network.

Old prejudices die slowly. Local fishermen still treat smallmouth bass with disdain. Even the esteemed walleye plays second fiddle to the native lake trout, especially during winter. To the local, hardy, Scandinavian descendants, the lake trout is prized both on the line and on the table. When the deep, rocky-bottom lakes of Gunflint-Trail country are covered with ice, local anglers fish for lake trout with deceptively simple techniques developed over several generations.

One of those locals is Kelly Shepard of Grand Marais. A native of the North Shore, Kelly likes to hunt and fish. In addition to working fulltime, he guides. During spring and summer, he specializes in brook trout, walleyes and lakers. In the fall, it's chinook salmon, black bear and deer. When winter comes, he takes several anglers ice fishing for lake trout.

Shepard has a reputation for catching fish, but he lacks the spit-and-polish of a typical professional fisherman. His blue parka looks as though it could go fishing by itself. (In fact, a bear stole his last fishing jacket off of a clothesline!) Aside from an ice auger and a jigging stick, Shepard's tackle will fit in a parka pocket. There are two reasons for this. First, many lakes he fishes are within a wilderness area where motorized travel isn't allowed. Second, in the 20-plus years he has been fishing for lake trout, he's honed his tackle selection to the bare essentials.

You can always tell where Shepard or other Gunflint locals have been fishing, because you'll see twigs sticking up from the ice. At first you might think these sticks merely mark fishing holes so no unlucky angler steps into a snow-covered hole. However, in an area where ice is 2 or 3 feet thick, soft spots usually aren't a concern until late in the season. Instead these sticks are remnants of homemade tip-ups. Shepard learned this special technique from his father.

Twig Tip-Up For Lake Trout

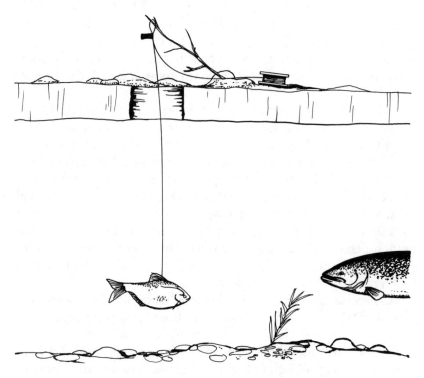

This is how Shepard's twig tip-up works. The secret to its successful operation is the use of a live, limber twig. Then the twig will function as a spring bobber.

"I started fishing with my dad when I was really young," he says. "Back then we could go into the BWCA with snowmobiles. I think dad brought us kids along just so he could bring back an extra limit."

This northwoods tip-up is simple to make. All you need is a spool of line, a hook, enough weight for your bait and a roll of plastic tape. Break off a limber branch from a lakeside bush. Push the branch into the snow beside your fishing hole. Lower your bait to the depth you intend to fish. Then make a loop in your line and hold it in place with tape folded so it sticks to itself. Hang the loop on the branch so it will slide off when a fish takes the bait. Unlike a tip-up whose flag flies when you get a bite, this system's tip-off is the tape's disappearance. Face the branch into the wind, however, to prevent accidental blow-offs. Shepard feels this method is superior to a standard commercially produced tip-up.

"I prefer using sticks instead of tip-ups," he says, "especially when the fish are biting light. With a tip-up, a trout has to strike hard enough to trip the flag or you won't know you have a bite. If you use a limber branch, you'll see it bend, like a spring bobber, even though the fish isn't hitting hard enough to pull the line off the stick."

Although lake trout are known to strike with the subtlety of starved piranha, especially during winter, they can be finicky at other times. The branch tip-up allows the line to slide down into the hole with virtually no resistance. If the fish does make a run, the spool (a typical, flat "filler" spool) will spin freely on the snow next to the hole. To make sure this will happen, Shepard will peel off about 10 feet of line to be sure it isn't frozen and then wind it back on the spool. He places the spool where it will catch on the branch before sliding down the hole. He and other locals tell of inattentive fishermen who didn't notice they had a fish on until it had run all the line off the spool.

Lakers can also be line shy. Although individual fish weighing 20 pounds or more swim in most lakes, the average Gunflint country lake trout weighs less than 5 pounds. Shepard prefers to use 6- or 8-pound-test monofilament line, light enough to fool a wary trout and strong enough to handle a big one. His favorite hook for lakers is a No. 6 Mustad egg-hook.

"I'm not a fan of oversized hooks," he says.

He is, however, a fan of ciscoes for bait. These small, silvery fish—known also as herring or tullibee—are a common forage species in many Northern lakes. You can find packages of frozen ciscoes in bait shops throughout the area. Similar in size to rainbow smelt, and a popular treat for lake trout, ciscoes are a better choice, Shepard says. They're more durable than rainbow smelt and easier to keep on a hook. Also, ciscoes are oilier; they release more trout-attracting scents into the water. He prefers to use ciscoes that are about 6 inches long. He also enhances their natural scent with a few drops of Dr. Juice.

Shepard has several methods for still-fishing with ciscoes. His favorite is suspending a cisco a foot or two from the bottom. The trick is getting the dead cisco to hang horizontally like a live fish. This is a must because lake trout avoid baits with an unnatural appearance. Shepard runs the hook through the cisco's back be-

Hooking A Cisco For Stillfishing

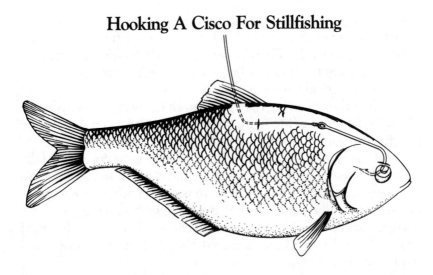

This is how Shepard hooks a cisco in order to present a realistic bait to very selective fish. The hook is pushed through the cisco below its dorsal fin, and then the hook is embedded at the back of the head.

neath the dorsal fin. Then he pulls the hook forward and inserts it at the skull's base.

"You get a good balance that way," he says. "Once you've hooked it, drop the cisco into the hole and see how it looks. Make it as natural as possible. Always hook a cisco near the head because lake trout swallow baits head-first."

If the suspended bait doesn't produce, Shepard lays a dead cisco on the bottom. Lake trout scavenge dead baits. Sometimes he'll combine live and dead baits using a cut cisco teamed with a shiner or sucker minnow. He'll make a diagonal cut from the cisco's dorsal to anal fin and use the tail section. The live minnow is hooked just beneath its dorsal fin. The struggling minnow gives action to the cisco tail which should be hooked just behind the dorsal fin.

"Always hook the minnow first and then put on the cut bait," Shepard says. "Otherwise a trout can pull the minnow off."

If Shepard is still-fishing with live bait only, he always uses two minnows for greater action. Both minnows should be hooked below the dorsal fin.

Lake trout and northern pike take a bait in the same manner.

Usually they make a short run before stopping to eat the bait. Shepard lets the fish take line. When it stops, he tightens the line until he feels the fish. Then he sets the hook. However, there are times when trout will just "play" with the bait, perhaps not even pulling the tape off the twig.

"When they're biting light, hit 'em right away," Shepard says. "Usually, I hold the line in my hand. When the fish pulls enough to bring my hand down to the water, I set the hook."

Few fish are more susceptible to a jigging action than lake trout. Minnesota ice fishermen are allowed two lines, so Shepard often jigs one line while still-fishing with the other. Some days, one method will outproduce the other. Jigging also is a good way to cover an area quickly, because you can work several holes until you find fish. Shepard uses a graphite ice rod and a spinning reel spooled with 6- or 8-pound-test.

"My favorite jigs are small airplanes weighing $\frac{1}{16}$ to $\frac{1}{4}$ ounce," he says. "Different jigs seem to work better than others on different lakes."

Airplane jigs have a circular action. Shepard recommends using a soft, smooth jigging action. Airplanes should be worked slowly. Lift once and then drop your rodtip. The airplane jig will make a lazy spin and then settle to a stop.

"If you jig too fast, the fish will not be able to catch up with the bait," he says.

Variations in your jigging pattern trigger strikes. Shepard likes to let his jig occasionally bounce on the bottom. He'll also bring his jig to rest about 18 inches above the bottom. With practice, you can learn to make your jig plane away at an angle. Usually, lake trout will strike when the jig is at rest or when you start to move it.

"More often than not, all you'll feel is some weight on the line," Shepard says. "The hard hits are usually smaller fish."

Concentrate your jigging efforts within 4 feet of the bottom, yet don't be afraid to try other depths. Sometimes you'll find lake trout cruising just beneath the ice. Start at the bottom and slowly work your jig to the surface. Lake trout are notorious followers. To draw a strike, you sometimes have to provide action that makes the bait appear to be alive and struggling.

Although the airplane is Shepard's standby, he uses other jigs. Another favorite is the Swedish Pimple. Again he recommends a

Airplane jigs are the mainstay of Shepard's ice fishing arsenal, and they are extremely effective on lake trout (as shown here). Shepard recommends a slow, methodical jigging action.

slow, methodical jigging action, pointing out that many anglers fish a Pimple too fast. He moves the rodtip in a figure-eight pattern. In some lakes, casting spoons can be the best producers. His favorites are Locos, Doctors, Fjords, Krocodiles and Little Cleos. Productive colors include silver, white and chartreuse. If you're not catching fish, try using different jig colors and types.

Shepard usually tips his jigs with minnows or cut bait. He replaces the manufacturers' trebles with single hooks which give better action to the bait. Also, it is more difficult to set treble hooks. A hook outside the fish's mouth can also get stuck in the ice when you bring the fish up through the hole. Of course, a cisco is his first choice for tipping a jig. However, if a lake has a large smelt population, he'll use the smelt as bait.

"Smelt fishing is a lot like fishing for crappies," he says. "We use a tiny jig tipped with a minnow tail or a very small minnow, and fish 15 to 20 feet down in about 50 feet of water. It's fast and furious when they're down there."

Finding lake trout on an ice-covered lake can be either easy or difficult, because the fish can be anywhere. However, Shepard has identified patterns that lakers follow during Minnesota's winter season, which is January through March. Early in the season, he looks for fish at a depth of 20 feet, usually near visible structure such as a point or a reef he found on a previous fishing trip. As the season progresses, trout move to areas 30 to 40 feet deep. As winter wanes in March, they move into the shallows. On one lake, Shepard has found hungry lakers chasing smallmouth bass fingerlings on rocky flats less than 10 feet below the surface.

"Have patience," he says. "Keep moving until you find fish and don't expect to slaughter them every time you go out. When I'm after lake trout, I plan to be out there all day."

A day-long diehard like Shepard has an advantage over most fair-weather fishermen. Lake trout action can be on again, off again. You may fish for several hours without a bite and then have a half-hour flurry of action. Shepard believes this may be related to subtle weather changes such as shifts in wind direction. Although he says he can't remember the last time he was skunked while fishing for lake trout, he prefers overcast days with a light wind. He also believes that lake trout are extremely sensitive to light and may be put off by daylight shining down through a fishing hole.

"Think about it," he says. "These fish have been living in darkness for several months, and then you start punching holes. These lakes are clear, and that light may penetrate about 20 feet or more."

Shepard also avoids making excessive noise when he's on the ice. On the few occasions when he uses a snowmobile, he turns it off when he arrives and doesn't start it again until he's ready to leave. He has noticed that trout often don't begin to bite until the area has settled down after the holes have been augered and lines set. He avoids walking around on the ice and, when still-fishing, will even go so far as to stand on shore.

"Of course," he says, "that depends upon the conditions. When there's 3 feet of ice it probably doesn't matter as much."

He also wonders about the impact that fishing pressure has on the fish. On some lakes there are areas traditionally popular with ice fishermen. He feels that although those hotspots remain productive year-in and year-out, the bigger fish shy away. His strategy is to try places away from crowds.

Are there places in a lake where he won't fish?

"Not necessarily," he says. "Generally, I'll stay away from shallow areas with a mud bottom or places where I've seen weeds growing in the summer. But don't be afraid to try anything. You've got to be willing to move in order to catch these fish consistently."

Hooking lake trout and landing them are two different things. Novices often lose fish that more experienced anglers would ice. Playing a lake trout requires finesse. Even a 4-pound fish can break 6-pound test if you don't give line when it makes a run. Lake trout fight twice as hard when you get them near the hole, a factor that may support the sensitivity-to-light theory. This is when most lakers are lost. If the fish wants to make a run, let it. Eventually the fish will tire. Guide it to the hole and bring it up head first, making sure not to catch the line on the hole's edge. Never lift a fish from the hole by the line. Instead, grasp the trout behind the head. With a good-sized fish, you should have a partner grab it while you control the line. Shepard carries a gaff when fishing on lakes where he might catch a trophy, but he rarely uses it.

Shepard doesn't consider himself an extraordinary lake trout fisherman. "Lots of guys know how to catch lake trout," he says. However, those Gunflint country ice fishermen with their twig tip-ups may know something else—something a technology-crazed fishing public has forgotten. The word *angling* is defined as trying to catch fish with a stick and a line length. In the complex world we live in, such simplicity is a treasure.

18

West Coast River-Run Salmon

by John Higley

almon are in! It happens every fall on many rivers up and down the West Coast. The arrival of the first wave is eagerly awaited by river anglers and the excitement builds to a fever pitch shortly after the first few fish are caught. The news is difficult—no, impossible—to contain and soon bank anglers and boaters are shoulder to shoulder and hull to hull in all the popular spots. For a while salmon are definitely in the spotlight, and anglers come from near and far to try their hand at catching their dream fish.

Two different salmon commonly enter West Coast streams: chinook (or king salmon) and the smaller coho (or silver) salmon. Because of their large size and wide distribution, chinooks are the salmon of choice for most anglers. Silvers, which are also widespread, offer good sport on some coastal streams; however, the kings provide more action overall. Thus, kings are the focus here, and the fishing techniques described apply mainly to them (although silvers are caught occasionally with the same tactics). (Incidentally, to tell the two subspecies apart, other than by size, look at their gumline. The gums of the coho's lower jaw are white to gray while the king's gums are generally black. Also, kings usually have spots on both the upper and lower tail lobes while silvers have spots only on the upper portion.)

There is magic and mystery in the very thought of salmon. Like Canada geese to a hunter, salmon symbolize the very heart of wildness to most anglers who pursue them with rod and line. Born

This fall-run salmon, displayed by guide Dave Schwabel, was taken from the Sacramento River. Schwabel has specialized in guiding anglers to king salmon in many West Coast rivers.

West Coast River-Run Salmon   205

in rivers and streams, these anadromous fish normally spend only a few months in freshwater before they enter the sea as smolts. They remain in the ocean from two to six years before returning to freshwater to spawn and die, thus completing their life cycle. Amazingly, this fish travels thousands of miles in the sea and uses a highly developed sense of smell to find the stream of its birth. Unfortunately some salmon runs have been adversely affected by man. Subject to all types of predation in the open sea, the fish are impacted even more by dams on home streams, which often block them from reaching miles of critical spawning habitat.

In order to mitigate spawning-ground loss, coastal states have built hatcheries on many streams; however, not all runs have fared well under the new regime. Through shortsightedness shown during early dam-building days, some runs were lost altogether, and others are dwindling even today. Despite the troubles, however, salmon remain plentiful, and anglers from San Francisco Bay to Alaska still look forward to the salmon's clockwork-like return each fall.

Most runs vary considerably in duration depending upon spawning-ground locations. On some streams, most salmon are present only for a few weeks at a time; on others, like the Sacramento River in northern California, the salmon runs may continue for much of the fall. It is a complicated agenda, needing an intricate regulations structure to manage the diverse runs.

The fighting characteristics of salmon in saltwater are legendary, but even in rivers, salmon are terrific battlers on hook and line. That, plus their large size, is why anglers enjoy fishing for them so much. Steelhead, which also have a large following, are smaller than salmon on average, but they're more apt to fight on top and become airborne. Chinook salmon may indeed jump; however, most of the time they conduct a bulldog battle in the holes. More than one angler has had to follow a monster king downstream hundreds of yards before finally bringing an end to the contest.

It's not unusual for small, precocious males (commonly called "jacks") to accompany a run. Returning after only a year in saltwater, jacks generally weigh only 2 to perhaps 5 pounds and measure less than 22 inches. While adult silvers may occasionally weigh as much as 15 pounds, adult kings are brutes, ranging in size from 12 to 40 and even 50 pounds, with the average somewhere

Schwabel mans the net as a client fights a salmon on the Klamath River. Schwabel prefers a double-ended MacKenzie-style drift boat for tracking and challenging these kings.

around 18 pounds. Some kings exceed 50 pounds. In 1979, O.H. Lindberg hooked and landed an 88-pound chinook salmon on California's Sacramento River, and that behemoth still is a state record.

Salmon feed voraciously in the ocean, but biological changes soon take place as they begin their upstream migration with the fish ceasing to eat in freshwater. The instinct to feed is still there, however, and anglers such as longtime river guide Dave Schwabel have developed some very effective ways to catch the fish with rod and reel. Surprisingly, though, it seems as if there are certain techniques unique to each geographic location which isn't to say that a bait or lure that works well in your backyard won't work just as well somewhere else. Often it's a simple matter of adapting a particular technique to the circumstances at hand.

Schwabel is a fulltime fishing guide with extensive experience in northern California and many other West coast locations. A native of northern California, the robust redhead, who has fished professionally for more than 25 years, began fishing for salmon with his grandfather in Washington on Puget Sound. Although he's never fished north of the lower 48 states, he has fished several

Oregon rivers, the Smith, Klamath and Eel rivers of the California coast and the state's primary inland salmon river, the Sacramento.

Dave's salmon fishing is largely done from a boat when he guides. On some coastal streams, he uses a double-ended MacKenzie drift boat. Inland, on the Sacramento, his newest fishing platform is a V-8 powered, 20-foot jet boat that easily gives his clients access to productive water that is along several miles of this major waterway.

"Bank fishing is certainly effective on some streams," Dave explains, "but at best you are limited to certain spots in a situation where the fish may move out at anytime. With a drift or jet boat, you can obviously cover lots of potentially productive spots in a day and keep moving until you find the fish."

Because of salmon fishing's popularity, there's plenty of competition among anglers today—with or without boats. An important part of fishing enjoyment, Schwabel says, is etiquette and boat safety. Assuming that you can run your boat skillfully while others are jockeying for position all around you, there's still the matter of fishing effectively and actually catching some fish.

According to Schwabel, most river guides use similar but varied tackle and techniques for different streams. It's often a matter of experience and persistence that makes the difference between a mediocre and a successful day on the water. Schwabel has strong opinions, but his understanding and love of fishing are apparent whenever the conversation revolves around piscatorial matters.

River salmon can be caught with various lures and bait. At one time or another, Schwabel has used all the local favorites including colorful lures such as the Okie Drifter, Li'l Corky, Spin-N-Glo, Birdy Drifter, Glo Balls and spoons and spinners with a silver, gold or bronze flash to them. Occasionally he fishes coastal waters with flies such as the Comet, Golden Comet and Fall Favorite. (These are usually fished near the bottom on a sink tip or straight, sinking fly line.) Schwabel says that many coastal drift fishermen rely mainly on Hot Shot and Wee Wart plugs. However, techniques and lures that have been used for decades on the Sacramento have spread recently, with terrific success, to the coastal rivers of California, Oregon and Washington, and north as far as Alaska's Kenai River.

Bait includes whole or portions of anchovies, gobs of cured roe

A sardine fillet or "wrapper" as it is called on the West Coast adds scent to the large Flatfish lure. This setup which first appeared on the Sacramento River is being used on many West Coast rivers.

and even balls of oil-packed, canned tuna wrapped in cloth mesh. Salmon may not be able to eat in freshwater, but Dave Schwabel reasons that because the instinct is still there, the scent factor plays a vital part in triggering strikes. Aggravation, especially in the case of some lures, also may be a contributing factor.

"The way we fish guarantees a lure flashing right in front of a salmon's nose," Dave says, "and it must be annoying as heck after a few minutes. I have no doubt that the salmon eventually lash out at what could be perceived as another fish which is invading their territory."

One of Schwabel's favorite Sacramento River techniques, and one that is now spreading north, is backtrolling with large silver or gold Flatfish (sizes T-50, T-55 or T-60) or similar Kwikfish (sizes K-14, K-15 or K-16) with a sardine fillet attached, flesh-side out, to the lure's bottom with thread. Locally this is called a sardine wrapper, and the idea is to add long-lasting scent to a lure. The effectiveness of such a rig isn't questioned by anglers familiar with its use. Backtrolling lets the lure work through a hole slowly with the current keeping tension on the line.

"Most of the time you want your lure to work right off the bottom," Schwabel advises, "and you've got to add some weight a few feet up the line. I install a three-way swivel 3 or 4 feet above the lure and clip the lead to a snap swivel on a 6- or 8-inch, monofilament dropper. Most of the time I use 20-pound-test line and a lighter dropper so I can break the sinker off if it's snagged. Everything varies, of course. If we're into really big fish that are basically breaking the line with their teeth during the fight, I use a 40-pound-test leader because it lasts longer. As for weight, it naturally varies from run to run. Sometimes I use 2 ounces or so, but in heavy current and deep water on the Sacramento I use a cannonball sinker weighing as much as 12 ounces. On most coastal streams, a lighter, pear-shaped bank sinker usually does the trick."

Just to be different, though, Dave tries backtrolling Flatfish plugs without adding weight to take them down.

"If the water isn't too deep, going weightless is fine," he says. "I've caught several fish that way that didn't seem to be hugging the bottom and it sure minimized snags." In lieu of lead, he occasionally uses a Luhr-Jensen Jet Diver to pull the lure down as far as 18 feet, with good results. Dave adjusts the lure size according to the individual situation, and he generally favors smaller plugs on coastal streams.

"To tell the truth," he says, "I like to fish with bait almost as much as with lures. On some days, cured roe is deadly while the fish ignore plugs. On other days, though, the reverse is true. You've got to experiment a bit to find out what the fish prefer at the moment."

Dave's standard technique is to install a sliding sinker on the line about 3 to 6 feet ahead of the roe, depending on water clarity, and to bounce the bait through a run by raising and lowering the rodtip a few inches at a time. This allows the current to move the bait a bit as the rodtip drops. You can do this in a power-controlled back drift with the bait directly downstream from the boat or by drifting alongside the bait at the same speed or by dragging the roe downstream behind a drifting boat. The idea is to feel

Welcome to the party! A number of boats jockey for position at daybreak in a popular salmon-holding run on a West Coast river. Sometimes the good spots are already taken.

the weight touch the bottom and to retrieve or release line as the current or depth changes. Some days, Schwabel says, the fish prefer a fast bounce which he provides by using less weight. As always, it pays to experiment.

It's important to keep the bait on the bottom where most of the fish are holding. For the sliding rig, he hangs a barrel swivel on the main line; then he joins the line and leader with another barrel swivel. The dropper is attached to the sliding swivel, and a snap swivel is attached to the end, allowing a quick weight change whenever necessary.

These days his roe hooks of choice are laser-sharp Siwash hooks, usually made by Eagle Claw or Owner, and tied with roe loops which make changing the bait a snap. Hook size is usually dictated by state angling regulations; Schwabel uses the largest legal size.

"We have used treble hooks and wrapped the roe on with thread," Dave says, "but roe loops are just as good and they're really easy to use. If I run into short strikers (which happens sometimes), I tie a smaller trailer hook to the roe hook and let it dangle 2 or 3 inches behind. Salmon don't know what a hook is, so the

Roe bait is often a good choice. In this case, a female king salmon from a West Coast river fell victim to this enticing bait. The roe must be cured so that it can be a durable bait.

fact that it's visible isn't a problem."

Cured, not fresh, roe is a must for bait durability. Most anglers can make their own cured roe from a fresh skein of eggs. Schwabel says there are several premixed cures on the market these days, and they work well; however, if you prefer to start from scratch, you can.

("Lay the roe out flat and split it down the center, then turn it upside down and let it drain until it feels tacky," Schwabel advises. "Then rub salt or white sugar, or both, into the eggs with your hand. Be sure to work it in well, then do the same with borax [about three parts borax to one part salt/sugar] and place the skein on a covered, non-metallic tray in the refrigerator for two or three days. It toughens enough for fishing in that time and retains good, natural color. Cut the bait from small roe pieces, and keep the rest cool until you need it.")

Whole anchovies also are especially effective near river mouths as the fish enter freshwater, and Schwabel uses them often. "I've caught salmon in sluggish water by simply sinking an anchovy down to the bottom and letting it sit there," Dave says. "But usually I back-bounce a whole anchovy downstream almost like roe. One time, though, I slow-drifted anchovies downstream on the Trinity River on light line weighted with a single, large split shot. The fish hit light so I set the hook at the slightest twitch. I caught and released 26 kings that day!"

Not surprisingly, Dave has definite thoughts on what tackle to use and when.

"For pulling plugs I like the feel of a medium action 8½-foot, glass rod like the Fenwick 85-C," says Dave. "It has some give and doesn't tend to jerk back when a fish hits. I think it gives my clients an extra instant to react and set the hook before the fish feels too much tension. On the other hand, I stick with a fast-action, 7-foot, graphite rod like Fenwick's Triggerstik for bouncing bait with a heavy weight. It takes a shorter stroke to lift the weight and set it down again, and it really makes a difference to a fisherman's

River-run king salmon are exciting to catch. This salmon puts on quite an acrobatic display on its way to the boat. The angler has to play the fish correctly in order to prevent break-offs.

Schwabel nets a rambunctious salmon for a client. Even netting salmon is something of an art form. Let the fish head into the net; don't try to net the fish from behind.

arm during a long day on the water. My rods also have just enough of a handle to provide some leverage for fighting a big fish but not so much as to be in the way in the boat."

Salmon are hefty fish and prone to long runs, so Dave uses nothing but levelwind reels with smooth, dependable drags and enough capacity to hold at least 225 yards of 20-pound-test line. There are several adequate reels available, of course, but Schwabel's own reels are well used Abu Garcia Ambassdeur 6500C's.

"I've seen hot fish smoke more than one reel," Dave says. "I won't name two popular brands that froze up on me, but I want quality tackle at every turn."

There are a couple of additional points to cover, namely finding the fish initially, landing the fish you hook and prime fishing times. As an aid to locating salmon, Schwabel has installed a

Complete Angler's Library

graph recorder on his boat. While salmon do hold in certain locations each season (you can tell by the cluster of boats), the graph comes in handy when the fish are on the move. When you find such a spot temporarily filled with fish, you usually have it to yourself, and even a short run can produce a fish or two.

As for landing hooked fish, Dave cautions against acting too soon. "Don't try to net a fish until you get its head up to the surface. Then come at it from the front—never the rear! If you try to net a salmon when it's still below the surface, the water's drag slows your swing, and chances are good that the fish will kick in the after-burner and take off again. If you're not expecting another burst of energy, you might pop the fish off before you get things under control."

Salmon may decide to bite almost anytime, Dave says, but 90 percent of the time the best bite of the day comes at daybreak, before most anglers are on the water stirring things up. Late afternoon is also a good time, and some days the bite really turns on just before dusk.

Obviously, there are many more ways to catch West Coast river salmon. However, the techniques used by Dave Schwabel and other guides have proven to be the most productive for these professionals over the long haul. Learn and use them under similar circumstances, and enjoy some of the best salmon angling.

Muskies And
Northern Pike

19

Open-Water Muskies

by Milt Miller

Bleeping repeatedly, the LCR's fish alarm indicated activity at the 18- to 28-foot level while guide Joe Bucher rigged up various lines and maneuvered his boat along a 39-foot-deep flat. A late-morning start on this exceptionally cold, single-digit, November morning stimulated his customers' anticipation on their initial trolling pass of the day. However, the wait wouldn't be long—no more than 15 minutes, tops. Bucher was still setting out lines when a slight turn in the boat's path triggered the first strike. The starboard line rigged off a planer board at 18 feet doubled.

The planer board did not release nor slide down the line like one normally would. Instead, it remained locked in position, even with the tremendous tension created by the pull of the boat's momentum against the weight of whatever size fish was hanging onto the other end. As Bucher revved the outboard throttle, the muskie battled fruitlessly against the boat's steady pull. Within a short time a 42-incher, scaling a healthy 21 pounds, was boated, photographed and released.

With only one line out and the boat still on the move, Bucher made a strong turn back toward the landmarked open-water area that so quickly produced the day's first muskie. Bucher's clients, now cranked with anticipation, reset the other planer-board outfit rigged with the same perch-colored, deep-diving crankbait and began letting out a couple of "deep set" wire-line outfits also rigged with deep divers. But as they approached the hotspot and

This 40-pound brute was suspended about midway in over 60 feet of water when it encountered guide Joe Bucher's precision trolling system. It was taken at 32 feet, just above the summer thermocline.

Open-Water Muskies 219

the sonar's fish alarm sounded once more, the same planer-board rig went off almost immediately. The battle began the same way with Bucher hitting the throttle and a customer grabbing the bent rod. Matters quickly became complicated when a second rod, this time a deep set, throbbed from a more powerful strike.

A "double"—two fish on at the same time—is almost unheard of, yet it was happening and within the first hour of fishing. The "board fish," a smaller muskie about 33 inches or so, quickly tired from the tug-of-war with the boat and the planer board's dead weight. It gave up in short order and was easily landed, unhooked and released. The deep-striking fish was another story.

Little ground was gained on this battler even during the tussle with the smaller muskie. The reel's drag begrudgingly gave out line in steady, short bursts, while the determined fish stayed deep. It struck the crankbait at about 28 feet and held at this depth throughout the battle. Nearly 10 minutes went by before a bulging 48½-incher succumbed to the landing net. With the motor still running, Bucher pulled out a digital hand-held scale and hooked it onto the landing net at a predetermined spot. "Minus the net weight, this one's a solid 34-pounder! What a beauty!" he shouted. Bucher's customer showed his excitement with a bellowing "Ya Hoo!"

What's unique about this story is that a single muskie is supposed to be difficult to catch, yet Bucher and his clients caught three muskies in less than an hour. Skeptics might argue that this was a once-in-a-lifetime occurrence, yet hundreds of witnesses claim Bucher is able to accomplish similar muskie feats consistently. He annually boats anywhere from 150 to 225 muskies per season and averages two muskies per trip (a day).

Annual big-muskie contests held across northern Wisconsin are usually stacked with either Bucher's name or that of several of his regular customers. Since he began guiding in 1976, Bucher has made his name synonymous with *big muskies*. Recently, Bucher took first and second place in Wisconsin's most heralded muskie contest, The Vilas County Musky Marathon. Both fish measured over 50 inches long. A guiding client's name appears in the 4th, 5th and 8th places. So, for just this contest alone, Bucher-related catches accounted for five of the top 10 places. Figuring conservatively that at least 25,000 anglers, novice and expert alike, wet a line for muskies in Vilas County, this one-year domination

Planer boards are a good way of covering more area while you're trolling. The boards increase the overall spread on each trolling pass and present the lure to boat-shy muskies.

alone in a major competition is incredible.

Bucher is quick to point out that first, it's those traditional myths and theories that make catching fish more difficult for most muskie chasers. "If you truly believe all that stuff about the muskie being a once-in-a-lifetime fish or the fish of 10,000 casts," Bucher says, "then it probably will be just that. As great as muskies are, most anglers simply overestimate them. They certainly are not as difficult to catch as most claim."

Second, it has been widely written for nearly a half-century that muskies are loners. The schooling, or "grouping instincts," common in most other fish varieties simply doesn't exist in muskies (it was thought). The muskie was a lone wolf who chased all other predators out of its territory. Yet Bucher claims that muskies regularly group up to feed. In fact, he calls them "wolfpacks."

Muskies can be loners, Bucher says, but a lot depends upon the terrain and the availability of baitfish.

Summer muskies in some Canadian lakes may be loners because they often hang around small pieces of cover, such as a big boulder or a tiny weed clump off the tip of an island. But, more often than not, these fish travel in wolfpacks of from three to five fish. Areas with a huge food supply might hold even larger wolfpacks of muskies, he says. "The biggest wolfpack of muskies I ever encountered contained at least 11 fish, but I'm certain there were a lot more," Bucher recalls. "We caught those 11 muskies but also lost several others. This all happened on one spot in a time span of only a few hours. Sizes ranged from 29 to 50 inches."

Another myth that Bucher and his customers regularly dispel is that big lunker-sized muskies don't feed in the same area with smaller fish. On the contrary, Bucher claims that muskies have evolved into an open-water fish partially because of increased fishing pressure. "Today, muskie fishermen hit the water in far greater numbers," he says, "and are much better equipped. Big muskies that frequented breaklines in hard-fished waters throughout most of the United States have simply been caught. Any trophy-class muskies that still attempt to feed on these heavily fished areas are actually moving into a life-threatening situation. Lure after lure after lure comes through these classic spots. Everybody knows about them, and everyone fishes them on a regular basis. Bigger fish with superior survival instincts which have evolved through time simply avoid these spots."

A second reason for this tendency toward open water is related more directly to food. "Muskies of all sizes not only have more security in the open water, but there's plenty of food, too," Bucher says. "Whitefish, ciscoes, shad, trout, perch and crappies are but a sampling of their choices. Anytime there's a lot of open-water forage present in a water body, muskies are sure to suspend. I think there have always been plenty of suspended muskies. We just didn't know they were out there or how to fish for them," Bucher says. "There was simply no need to fish them years ago.

"Plenty of classic breakline muskies existed then," Bucher continues. "I'm simply adapting Great Lakes salmon trolling methods to take them. Find baitfish, troll different lures at various speeds, and—bingo—some muskies are likely to be caught."

Bucher's confidence in fishing suspended muskies gives the

impression that this is an almost "can't miss" technique. Yet he warns there's more to it than that: "Without question, a guy could simply troll a couple of lures behind the boat over open water and stumble onto a few muskies once in a while. But knowing approximate fish locations and using precision trolling techniques are the keys to really scoring consistently."

Bucher credits the late Bob Ellis, a northern Wisconsin row-trolling muskie fanatic, with turning him on to suspended muskies. "When I first started guiding in northern Wisconsin in the early 1970s, Bob Ellis was a local legend," he says. "He caught more big muskies out of a small rowing skiff than all the big-name muskie guides combined. He didn't even have a motor on his boat! I became close friends with Bob a few years before he died, and I'll never forget his words about big suspended fish. One of my favorites was, 'You can have all those muskies that hang around the weedbeds, rock points and sandbars. I'll take that one that swims over the deep, open water.' Another one of his unforgettable lines was, 'I know if there's any chance that a record-class muskie still lives in these hard-fished waters, it's bound to be suspended over open water where it lives undisturbed.' These were strong statements, but the one that really hit home with me was 'Just think, there are probably a lot of muskies living out there in the open water that have never seen a lure!'"

Ellis had convinced Bucher. "Now it didn't matter how many fishermen were on a lake pounding all the well-known spots," Bucher says, "because they weren't going to be fishing where I was. Now I had all this water to myself.

"It's kind of funny how differently I look at a topographical map of a new lake now," Bucher admits. "Instead of looking for shallow food shelves such as bays, big shoreline points and mid-lake humps, I purposely look for isolated deep holes or deep bottlenecks near two points. I even feel totally different about the way I look at a lake itself when I pull into the boat landing every day. Instead of scanning the lake quickly to see who's on all the over-fished hotspots, I simply look out at the middle of the lake and wonder just how big a fish is swimming out there over that open water. It sure opens up a whole new frontier."

Precision Trolling's The Answer

Although suspended muskies can be caught by casting, preci-

Precision Trolling System For Suspended Muskies

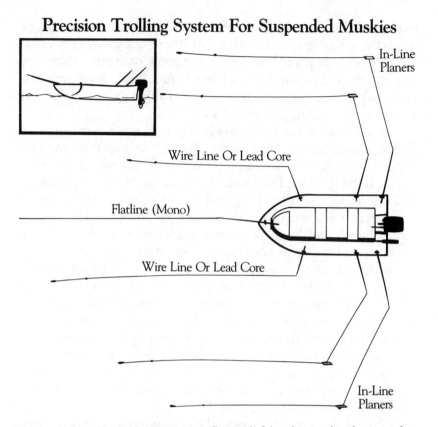

In-Line Planers

Wire Line Or Lead Core

Flatline (Mono)

Wire Line Or Lead Core

In-Line Planers

This is a diagram of Joe Bucher's precision trolling method for taking muskies that suspend in open water. What is unique about this system is that he does this while backtrolling.

sion trolling is the best method overall. A lot more water can be covered with greater efficiency. The caster can only check a fraction of the water that a troller can. Rig that troller up with multiple lines, and there's simply no contest.

Far greater depths can be reached by trolling than by casting. Even the deepest diving lures rarely get below 12 feet when they're cast. The same lure normally travels twice that depth when it is trolled. Add some additional weight, or attaches the lure to lead-core or wire line and all kinds of deep-diving opportunities abound. When muskies are suspended below 25 feet, specialized trolling setups are in order. This can all be handled quite easily with the proper equipment.

Another great trolling advantage, when the subject is suspended muskies, is being able to check various depths at the same time. When running multiple lines at various depths, one can quickly and efficiently strain potential water to find the productive depths. Then immediate adjustments can be made to all your lines in the "strike" zone.

This is basically what Bucher does when attacking suspended muskies. He trolls at least three lines per angler (permissible in Wisconsin). He prefers to fish with no more than two customers and a maximum of nine lines. Imagine nine lines being trolled at one time across a stretch of open water. If there's an active, suspended muskie out there, Bucher's sure to find it in short order.

Bucher's requirements for a boat, motor and sonar unit are very important to the success of this system. He prefers a 16- to 17-foot boat, powered by a medium-sized tiller outboard (25 to 50 horsepower). "I simply don't like big, high-performance rigs with steering consoles for this kind of fishing," he says. "I want to be able to turn the boat left or right on a dime and hit the throttle in an instant. A tiller-outboard enables me to do that, and all with one hand."

When the water gets real cold in the fall, Bucher says ultra-slow speed is the key to success. It's during this key big-fish period that Bucher prefers to backtroll his crankbaits so as to further reduce speed while he's still maintaining good boat control. "Try backtrolling with a steering console once and you see the need for the tiller-outboard right away," he says. "Trolling backward with a steering-wheel-controlled boat is tough in itself. Adjusting speeds quickly is nearly impossible."

Sonar units are also an integral part of Bucher's trolling arsenal. Any of the better-quality LCR units that contain a fish alarm and decent resolution are good. "The fish alarm is a big help, really," he says. "With it, I'm keenly aware of baitfish presence and the depth ranges where marks most frequently occur. I always try to run lures right at the top and bottom depths indicated by sonar signals. In other words, if I'm marking a lot of fish in the 15- to 32-foot range, I'm certain to set a few lines at 15 feet and some deep-sets at 32 feet. I've had some exceptional success lately while experimenting with the 3-D units. Because they display fish signals left, right or dead center of the boat, I can often predict which line is most apt to get a strike."

His boat also has an ample number of prerigged rod holders anchored at various opportune spots around the boat. Bucher prefers models with a female mount which can be anchored almost flush with the boat's gunwale. The business end of the rod holder fits into an adjustable gear-like mechanism. This rod-holder style can be easily adjusted both horizontally and vertically. When it's not being used, it can be removed and stored out of the way.

Bucher's rod-and-reel setups are top quality and fall into two categories, a planer-board rod and a deep, wire-line rod. For planer boards, Bucher uses a stout 9-foot rod and a large levelwind trolling reel, spooled with a 40- to 50-pound-test, saltwater-brand line. "The line is a key ingredient here," says Bucher. "Standard lines used by most anglers won't hold up to the constant pinching of the planer-board snubber. The snubber damages the line, and when a lunker hits—pop—there goes your trophy. Saltwater-brand line is stiff and very thick in diameter, but it's super tough. It doesn't scar from the planer-board snubber."

Bucher says 40- to 50-pound saltwater line is so tough that he doesn't have to use a wire leader for suspended muskies. "Muskies can surely bite line, even the heavy stuff, but I've never lost one to a bite-off with this saltwater stuff. In addition, minimal contact with obstructions occurs when you're open-water trolling. And when a muskie is hooked, you can destroy a muskie's ability to roll up on your line by simply kicking up the throttle. I pull on that fish with the outboard's power until it stops that initial, violent thrashing. If it starts to do it again later in the fight, I crank up on the outboard again. This stops the rolling almost totally."

On Bucher's deep-running rigs that he calls his "deep sets," he runs either lead-core line or solid wire. "Lead core has gained a great deal of popularity once again with walleye trollers because you get good depth control along with knowing exactly how much line you have out," he says. "However, solid wire line gets even greater depths than lead core. It's just more difficult to find and work with. If you get a backlash with this stuff, it's not a pretty sight. Plus, you have to have a meter on your reel or count the passes on the reel's levelwind in order to know how much line is out."

Bucher prefers 50-pound, solid, trolling wire attached to a strong black swivel with a haywire twist. Then he rigs a 4- to 5-foot leader of the same 40- to 50-pound, saltwater monofilament used on his board rods and ties the crankbait directly on it. This rig enables him to reach depths in excess of 40 feet with very little

Bucher doesn't mess around in dealing with muskies. He uses heavyweight tackle and big lures. He's found that saltwater-style line works best because of its diameter and weight.

Open-Water Muskies

line out. "The heavyweight wire line acts like a big sinker," he says. "I can get my crankbait to run 40 feet with minimum line out. You simply can't get this kind of depth control with any standard line. If you use real light line that some guys claim they do to get extra depth, you risk breaking off on a big fish too easily. I'd rather have 40- to 50-pound line on when a bruiser hits."

Although just about any deep-diving crankbait catches its share of muskies, Bucher's lure choice is very specific; he uses only a crankbait of his own design, called the DepthRaider. "I've used just about every muskie crankbait there is," he says, "and I've caught muskies on just about all of them, but I wanted something more out of a big-fish crankbait so I began making my own. Most muskie lures are made of wood. While wood is nice to work with and creates a nice lure action, it is not durable. Especially when muskies are the target. Muskies sink their teeth into wood, ruining the finish and making it much tougher to set the hooks. That's why I went to a high-impact plastic. I wanted the lure to last and the fish to take the hook."

His lure also has a double-reinforced, deep-diving lip that is molded into the bait. Bucher didn't want the lip to be a separate component attached by screws or glue. "With this design," he says, "the lip is the strongest, not weakest, part of the lure, and it's guaranteed never to go out of tune."

Crankbait colors that Bucher chooses for any given day depend largely upon light conditions and experimentation. He has found that green, perch-type patterns work in just about every kind of water. And although natural black-and-white sucker minnow patterns are popular, they haven't produced the same results as perch patterns. When muskies appear to want a white-bodied plug, which happens quite often in cold water, Bucher has had far better results with a cisco/shad-style pattern that features flashy white/silver sides and a bluish back. Under heavy overcast or any other low-light conditions, he relies heavily upon a very dark color pattern with black, gold or orange accents.

Once Bucher locates a possible open-water muskie haven, he begins setting up lines in a prescribed manner. "The first thing I do is get the board rods out," he says. "They're the toughest to rig initially, and once in place, they're out of the way. Reversing this process often leads to tangled lines. I must first decide how deep I want my board lures to run. Usually I start with one board lure

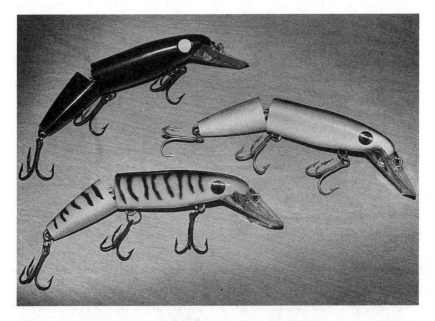

This is a sampling of Bucher's favorite trolling crankbaits for taking open-water muskies. He wasn't satisfied with commerical lures so he designs and builds his own, called DepthRaiders.

unweighted on one side. This covers the 12- to 15-foot-depth range. Because this lure runs about 40 to 60 feet of line out, I attach it tightly to an in-line planer board and then let the board out about 30 feet. I do not rig my boards in a breakaway manner. The slack line or tension reduction that results when a board pops off is all a muskie needs to shake the lure free. Constant tension is the answer to keeping muskies hooked on boards. I simply detach the board when it's retrieved to boatside. The first board rod is then placed in a rod holder pointing upward at nearly a 45-degree angle from the water."

When more depth is required from the board-rigged crank-baits, Bucher attaches a 1½-ounce rubber-core sinker on the line about 3 to 4 feet up from the crankbait. He says the additional 1½-ounce weight adds about 6 feet of running depth to the lure, putting it in the 18-foot zone. "This additional weight is critical when slow, fall trolling is attempted," the veteran guide advises. "The DepthRaider wobbles at a snail's pace, but does not dive at an ultra-slow speed because of its buoyancy. The 1½-ounce rubber-core sinker takes care of the depth control. Add two sinkers of this weight and you can put that lure down over 30 feet if enough line is let out behind the board."

Bucher also attaches special hooks to his planer board crankbaits to increase their hooking potential. Most anglers have no idea how critical hook design is to their hooking percentages, Bucher says. On top of that, some hooks work great for one situation but poorly for another. Bucher opts for a VMC 9649 in the 2/0 size for his particular crankbait whenever it's rigged off a planer board. "The VMC 9649 is the fastest penetrating treble hook available. This is essential for consistent hookups with muskies on boards. I've experimented with this system for a long time. The VMC hook is critical."

Once the board lines are in place, rigging the deep sets are the next step. Bucher has researched the running depths of his lures closely and determined exactly how deep they go versus the amount of wire line out. "Few people realize how much line length affects running depth," he says. "It's critical with any kind of line you use, but with wire it makes an incredible difference. For example, when I'm using 50-pound Monel wire, every pass of my levelwind adds about 2 feet of running depth to the lure. In other words, eight levelwind passes equals 16 feet deep, 16 passes equals 32 feet of running depth."

With this "2 feet per pass" concept, Bucher can fish precisely at any depth he chooses. When sonar readings indicate strong fish presence at 28 feet, for example, he simply counts out 14 passes and runs a lure right through these fish. Quick adjustments are easily made by turning the reel handle or releasing a few feet of line. Some of the newer trolling reels contain line meters which perform the same basic task. Once you've taken the time to chart the running depth of your lures, precision depth control is easily attained.

Bucher doesn't use downriggers, because he thinks they're simply unnecessary: "Why would you want to use a downrigger, when you can get precision deep-water depth control without one? Plus, when the lure is directly in-line, you can tell if it's working properly by watching the rodtip vibration. This is all negated with a downrigger. And if you want to bounce bottom, the downrigger's cannonball-weight constantly gets hung up." Perhaps the most important reason that Bucher doesn't use a downrigger for suspended muskies is that when the downrigger release pops free, too many fish are lost during the time it takes to pick up the slack line. "Unless muskies are working deeper than 50 feet," he says, "downriggers are simply more trouble than they're worth. Wire line gets most deep diving muskie crankbaits down to the 50-foot range fairly easily, and it's a lot simpler."

One of the more surprising aspects of Bucher's trolling system is his reaction to a strike. Instead of shutting the outboard down, Bucher maintains course with the outboard "on" and in gear. "If I keep the outboard on and in gear," he says, "it keeps all the other lines from fouling. I can also control the battle to a great degree by making turns or increasing the power as the fish tries to cut across lines or do any heavy thrashing."

A higher percentage of muskies stay hooked; Bucher claims he loses very few fish by maintaining course throughout the battle. Usually the only adjustments he makes are slight turns to compensate for the fish's lateral movements.

Another benefit of keeping all the lines on the move is, of course, the potential for additional strikes. Bucher's clients and regular fishing companions say they frequently encounter doubles. "Doubles occur once in a while, but what happens more frequently is another strike within minutes of landing the first fish," Bucher explains. Because all the remaining lines are still out there working, he and his clients lose little time rerigging and positioning the boat over high-potential water. Once these fish make their move, Bucher wants to take full advantage of every moment.

Trolling deep, open water for suspended muskies is but another piece of innovative angling. When lake conditions change and fishing pressure rises, big trophy-sized muskies head straight for the deep, open water. It offers both security and ample food. Using Joe Bucher's method of combining planer boards and deep, wire-line rigs is perhaps the most efficient way yet of taking these magnificent fish.

20

Jerkbait Pro

by Darl Black

Anglers who regularly fish the muskie lakes of Crawford County, Pennsylvania, recognize at a glance the lone figure tossing awkward-looking plugs. Maybe they have never been formally introduced, but they know his name—and his reputation. After all, it does not take long for word to spread about someone who lands 50 muskies a season.

The man is Dan Shay of Meadville, Pennsylvania. Shay is not a guide or professional fisherman. His fulltime employment only allows time for fishing on weekends and during vacations. Yet almost every season since 1975, he has caught at least 50 legal muskies (30-inch minimum) from many prime northwest Pennsylvania waters.

During good years, he has averaged between 65 and 80 fish. His best year was a record 105 legal fish! On three different occasions Shay has caught seven legal fish in one day; four times he has landed five muskies in one day.

Shay rarely keeps a fish. Only two muskie mounts adorn his den; the larger one is a 38-pounder. Being catch-and-release oriented, he does not weigh the muskies. However, using a length-to-weight conversion for typical muskies in Pennsylvania, he figures there have been not less than 20 fish in excess of 30 pounds. Two of those released fish weighed more than 40 pounds. Despite such success, Shay never set out to create a reputation; it just kind of happened.

His first muskie came from Cussewago Creek when he was 12.

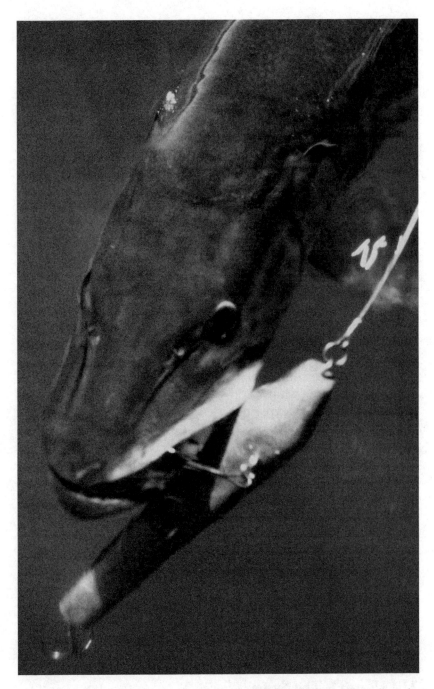

This muskie has just fallen victim to Dan Shay's special jerkbait technique. Shay's lure is his own design and homemade, but it's built so the fish can't pull the treble free.

Jerkbait Pro

Although only 30 inches long, the muskie made a memorable fish story for a youngster.

Fifteen years later, the muskie bug really bit. Tracking down those large, powerful, critters became an obsession. Shay trolled and cast crankbaits for muskies. His fishing playground included Pennsylvania's finest muskie waters: Conneaut Lake (which produced the 54-pound, state record muskie in 1928), Sugar Lake, Canadohta Lake, Cussewago Creek, French Creek, Allegheny River, Pymatuning Reservoir and Tamarack Lake.

By the 1980s he had gained local recognition as a successful muskie fisherman. Then one summer day in 1985, his approach to muskie fishing took an unforgettable turn.

"I was on Tamarack Lake, casting my usual lures," he said. "I observed an unfamiliar boat with a couple of guys who looked like they were seriously into muskie fishing. Every time I saw them, they seemed to be fighting, landing or releasing a fish. Being like I am, I sort of moseyed over.

"They had observed me release the two fish I had caught that day, so we got to talking. Turns out they were jerkbaiting and had taken 12 muskies between them. I looked at their baits which didn't seem to be complicated. I had a similar one in my box but really didn't know what to do with it. 'You got to jerk it with a good rod snap,' they explained.

"Thanking them for the advice," he continues, "I tied on the one from my box and started jerking it. Within minutes, I caught my first jerkbait muskie. From then on, I have used only jerkbaits."

That summer Shay caught and lost several muskies before he broke off his store-bought jerkbait. "It was all new to me back then," says Shay. "I had no one to help me or point out what I might be doing wrong. I didn't have the right line, the right reel or the right rod for jerkbaits. Rather than spend $7 to $10 for each new lure, I figured I could make my own."

It was trial and error. Using two different commercial baits as models, he started designing his own lures. Out of the first dozen jerkbaits he built from wood scraps, only one performed properly. Then he examined his rod, reel and line. Eventually, Shay worked out a jerkbait system, resulting in incredible catches.

The Heart Of The System

Shay uses two basic jerkbaits (both homemade) ranging in size

Pull Bait Action

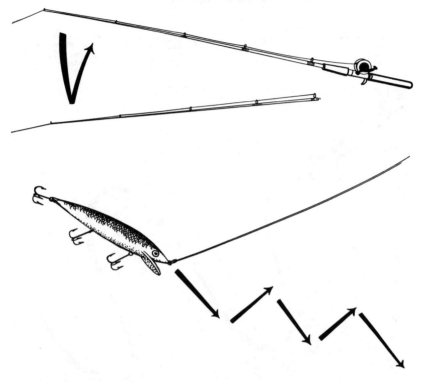

To make the pull bait work, the angler snaps the rodtip down and takes in line as the tip is raised again. This causes the bait to dive with the rod snap and rise when the slack line is taken in.

from 8 to 14 inches for his muskie-catching system.

He refers to his first design as a "pull" bait. It is a buoyant, diving jerkbait. "Pull baits work up and down," Shay explains. "The big lip coupled with the added weight digs the bait deep on the pull. When you give it slack line, the bait floats toward the surface. That movement, or jump, may be 2 to 4 feet depending upon the model."

His second design is based on glider-type jerkbaits. Shay refers to it as a "slide" bait. Unlike most similar commercial jerkbaits (when at rest), Shay's slide bait sinks as opposed to floating or remaining neutrally buoyant. "Slide baits work back and forth," he says. "It's like a dog-walking bait, only it runs underwater. I have slide baits that sweep as much as 6 feet one side to the other."

In developing his particular style of jerkbaiting, Shay experi-

Slide Bait Action

In using the slide bait, the angler pumps the rod in a circular motion, pausing at the bottom of the circle to allow the bait to slide. This gives a sideways action to the bait.

mented with various rods and reels. For working the pull bait, he stayed with a casting outfit. However, for the slide bait he chose a spinning outfit. The rods he uses are moderately priced, extra-tough, almost indestructible fiberglass series. His favorites include Berkley's P-16 Power Pole, a 6-foot casting rod, and Shakespeare's SP1100 Ugly Stik, a 6-foot spinning rod. Shay considers all-graphite rods too fragile for the frequent "rod against gunwale" contact which happens when jerkbaiting. And he figures if an angler can be successful with less expensive rods, why spend more money on high-priced equipment?

The most important tackle piece is the reel, says Shay. "You have got to have a reel which can stand up to hard use. I toss lures which weigh from 4 to 8 ounces. Few reels have been able to take the constant slapping of the line against the line guide and spool.

It's like the transmission in a car—if it breaks down, you are done. You can't fish with a reel that flies apart." Basic, quality reels like the Penn Mag 10 casting reel and Penn 450SS spinning reel are Shay's picks for durability and strength.

Line on the most frequently used baitcaster is 30-pound dacron, and a second reel has 50-pound test for use with the heaviest plugs. The spinning reels are filled with 20-pound-test, Ande monofilament. Wire leaders are made from .030 or .040 single-strand stainless-steel wire. The lighter leaders go on the smaller baits. One end of the leader is wrapped directly to the jerkbait. A barrel wrap on the opposite end allows the line to be attached with a heavy-duty interlocking snap swivel. The snap swivel on the line permits quick lure changes.

Putting Life Into The Lure

Unlike crankbaits and bucktails, jerkbaits have no automatic action when pulled through the water. The angler must manipulate rod and line to give life to a jerkbait. It is that spark which entices a muskie to strike.

"Muskies hit a jerkbait because of its erratic action," explains Shay. "It's the old story about looking like an injured baitfish; muskies find it hard to turn down an easy meal. Retrieve a crankbait or spinner past a non-feeding muskie and it will likely ignore it. But give it something that appears to be struggling and few muskies can resist it."

Shay's two types of jerkbaits have entirely different actions requiring different rod manipulations. "When I am working a pull bait, the rod is snapped hard straight down to force the bait to dive. The amount of weight added to the bait's head is a primary factor in how deep the bait will go.

"Following the downward stroke, the bait begins to float upward as slack line is taken up by the reel. Usually with pull baits, the rod is pounded downward again before the bait has a chance to reach the surface. The working depth varies from a couple feet to as deep as 5 feet, depending upon the amount of lead weight."

Shay prefers fishing a slide bait over the pull bait in most instances, and he has mastered its side-to-side glide motion through an unusual rod technique. Following a cast, the slide bait is counted down to a desired depth. Usually it is retrieved within 1 to 3 feet of the surface especially when worked over submerged vegetation. But on the edge of cover, Shay may count a slider down to 5 feet or deeper. His weighted baits usually hold the depth to which they were counted down. He considers 8 feet the maximum running depth for an effective retrieve.

"With a slide bait, I am reeling and pumping at the same time," Shay says. "It is a difficult technique to master. You are not turning the reel's handle to move the bait as much as you are turning the rod." The rod handle is tucked along the right forearm as the arm moves in a vertical, circular motion. Forward, down, back, and up—like turning a meat grinder. The left hand on the handle rotates in sync with the rod, while slowly turning the reel handle to pick up slack line. "All I do is make a circular motion with the rod," Shay says. "Let the rod do the work."

A slide bait swims or glides first in one direction, then turns and glides in the opposite direction. Some sliders are designed for short sweeps of 10 inches to 1 foot. Others are designed for much longer arcs. A short, round-head model has a quicker, shorter side-to-side movement. Long, narrow models offer a much wider side-to-side glide. The speed of the pumping motion is matched to a particular slide bait. Short sweeping baits require a faster circular motion, while wide sweeping baits are worked slower.

"With spinning gear I can make a slide bait do anything I want it to," says Shay. "I have more control over it. There is a knack— a certain coordination—which makes it work. But once you get the retrieve down, and use it with one of my lures, you will have a bait working in a manner that really stirs the interest of muskies.

"Muskies seem to have preferences depending upon the conditions. On dark days I want a bait which works about 1 foot back and forth. On bright days I have more success with slide baits which glide long distances, some up to 6 feet. Also, long glides are more effective in colder water," he says.

To get the longest gliding distance out of a slide bait, you let it coast after the pump. Watch where the line enters the water. When the line starts to sink, you know the bait has reached its maximum slide distance and is starting to drop. It's time to pump the rod again.

On Hooking, Landing And Handling

How far should one cast a jerkbait? Shay stresses that each individual must establish his own distance. "You have got to get

Shay whips his lure out over the water. He says anglers have to establish their own casting distance and develop a retrieve rhythm that "does not wear you out."

comfortable with a casting distance and a rhythm of retrieve which does not wear you out," he says. "Don't try throwing a heavy bait as far as possible on every cast—you won't be able to keep it up all day. It's like a baseball pitcher. He can't attempt to throw all fast balls as hard as possible for nine innings. You have got to pace yourself."

Shay has found that 90 percent of the strikes occur during two specific phases of a retrieve. A bait will be hit by a muskie either during the first 10 feet of a retrieve after splashdown or during the last 10 feet as it approaches the boat. Very few fish hit midway through a retrieve. It is often suggested that an angler figure eight on every cast, but Shay admits he doesn't.

"If I see a fish following, I will plunge the rodtip into the water and sweep it in a figure eight," he says. "It works about half the time. Many times I will figure eight even if I don't actually see a fish. It's just intuition that a fish may be there."

According to Shay, setting the hook on a muskie is not a problem. Then he adds, "If you keep sharp hooks, a muskie will practically hook itself. Give the rod a good snap upward, keep the line tight, the rodtip up, and hold on!" The drag should be set to permit the fish to take line. But you don't want the line to slip when setting a hook, nor do you want it so tight the line snaps.

"As I work a fish to the boat, I gauge its size and how hard it has been fighting to determine how much tension to put on the fish," he says. "Sometimes I may tighten the drag up as I work the fish in. This really is a bad habit to get into—monkeying with the drag while working a fish. I have been known to tighten the drag too much. But the reason is to get the fish in before it is completely tired out. I believe working a muskie to total exhaustion reduces its chances of survival."

Always attempt to release a muskie without removing it from the water. This procedure prevents injury to the fish and to the angler. With the fish resting at boatside, Shay grabs the engaged hook with a pair of lineman's pliers. Using a quick backward twist, he pulls the hook out. The barbs on his hooks have been squeezed down into a low profile when they were installed on the plug, thus making this unhooking method fairly successful. If the hook cannot be dislodged, he simply cuts it and replaces it with a new 2/0 or 3/0 treble. Sometimes a fish becomes hooked in such a way that it cannot survive. In the last 10 years, Dan has kept only 11 muskies; all but three of those were the result of hook injuries.

Making The Baits

When Shay started making his own lures, he tried several different woods but finally settled on cedar and maple. Buoyant cedar fit the bill for the pull baits which must rise toward the surface.

On the other hand, maple remained submerged when weighted which was the goal Dan sought in a subsurface slide bait. On the pear-shaped wooden slide baits the hook hangers were screwed in; but sometimes the screw's eyes were ripped out by fish. Repair work to the baits was ongoing. The water-saturated maple would crack and split after drying out over the winter.

Then two years ago Shay uncovered an industrial plastic used at his workplace. The three liquid parts—resin, hardener and fill-

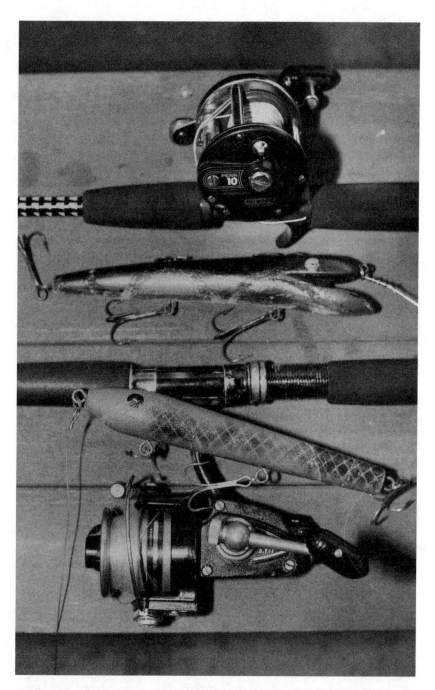

Shay's tackle includes (top) Penn Mag 10 reel and Power Pole with a pull bait, and (bottom) Penn 450SS reel on an Ugly Stik for use with a slide bait.

Jerkbait Pro

er—are combined to create an extremely durable plastic. A mold maker by trade, Shay made plug molds and used excess material from a job to pour baits.

Once the plastic was cured, hook attachment eyes could be screwed directly into the plug without fear of them being pulled out by a thrashing muskie. The plugs did not require hours of sanding, and the paint readily adhered to the surface. Lead was still added to the plug in holes drilled forward of the first hook, but the correct balance was easier to achieve with plastic.

The pull baits are still crafted from cedar because the plastic is not buoyant enough. Each one is drilled clear through from belly to the plug's flat back. A cotter pin is slipped through each hole, and the pins bent over. To set the pins in place, molten lead is poured in the front hole and epoxy fills the rear one. Slip rings are added to the eye of the pins. Lead is also poured in a nose hole to secure that line attachment cotter pin. The tail-hook pin receives epoxy. The amount of lead added determines the working depths.

Sharing Additional Secrets

Anglers would do well to note the color schemes used on Shay's jerkbaits. All pull baits are painted black, sometimes with a little red or silver added as accent. Shay is uncertain why he prefers solid black on pull baits. He does know, however, that it works. "Black is as good as anything you can use," he says.

But on slide baits he puts more effort into giving them a baitfish-like appearance. The object, however, is not to imitate any forage in particular and not to produce bright colors which are unnatural. He developed a painting scheme which gives the appearance of a shimmering baitfish in the water.

"I blend three different colors to get that reflective appearance on the slide bait's sides. First, I spray a coat of high gloss gold, then a coat of high gloss silver and finally a coat of flat gold overlay. It doesn't look like much out of water, but it glistens in the water."

Even though the gold finish is his all-around favorite, there is one additional color Shay would not be without. An orange-and-black blend works well on a few baits when a lake has an algae bloom. "When the lake turns funky green," Shay says, "the orange baits catch more muskies."

Most muskie anglers switch techniques throughout a season. Shay, however, stays with jerkbaits because it is so much fun.

Each year he takes fish from the opening day in May right up until Thanksgiving. He identifies two peak jerkbait times. The first one is the initial prolonged warming period in June until about mid-July. The second one kicks in from October to early November and usually produces the season's largest fish. He does acknowledge August is his lowest catch rate; some years he never catches a single muskie the entire month.

Shay realizes his technique is not productive for all water types. He limits his fishing to slow-moving creeks, shallow man-made impoundments with lots of cover and natural lakes with abundant deep weed flats. He knows that when muskies can move deeper, his chances of success are greatly reduced. Therefore, his favorite waters are shallow lakes with a lot of vegetation. Hope of a muskie over 50 pounds may be limited, but he discovered that jerkbaiting is much more exciting than dragging a plug for hours behind a boat.

Having disclosed his jerkbait system for muskies, Shay offers his final secret for success: "You aren't going to catch muskies sitting at home. You have got to put in the hours. I don't care who you are or how good you are, or how expensive your lures and equipment are, if you aren't on the water, you don't catch fish."

21

Finding Midsummer Pike

by Gary Clancy

D ick Gryzinski is his real name. So naturally, you assume that his nickname, "The Griz," is a shortening
of his last name. Makes sense until you meet the man.
Up swaggers a bearded giant of a man, with—honest
now—*silver-tipped* hair sticking up from his head just like the hack-
les on that distinguishing back-hump of a not-very-happy grizzly
bear. Before you can turn and run, he sticks out a paw the size of a
cast-iron frying pan and growls out something like, "Git your gear,
it's going to be a great day of fishing."

If a grizzly could talk, its voice would probably sound something like The Griz's, one-third gravel, one-third growl and one-
third roar. So, of course, you have to ask, "Hey Griz, how did you
get the name, anyway?"

"Don't know for sure. Doesn't matter much anyway. C'mon,
get your stuff, and let's go fishing."

Never mind that The Griz has been fishing every day for the
past 90 days. That enthusiasm you detect in his grizzly voice is
real. The Griz would be fishing today whether you, his customer,
had showed up or not. On the rare days when he does not have a
guide trip, The Griz simply goes fishing by himself. The man definitely lives to fish.

If someday you should go fishing with The Griz, let me give
you some advice. Take along a big lunch. No, not because The
Griz will wolf down most of it; he is much too intense to spend
much time eating when he is on the water. He can go for days on

The Griz lands a nice mid-summer pike. He constantly defies the popular notion that you can't catch big pike in the summer heat. He says it's a matter of giving them what they want.

Finding Midsummer Pike   245

a jar of peanut butter, some crackers and a bag of store-bought cookies which may have been in the boat since last season. No, you are going to need the nourishment, because you are going to be on the water all day. The Griz doesn't work a six- or even an eight-hour guide-trip. Try 10, 12, even 14 hours. He genuinely hates to see the sun go down.

"The Arctic Circle would be the perfect place to guide," The Griz says. "Up there, I hear they have 23 hours of sun every day. Man, could a guy catch fish then."

The Griz is one of those rare individuals who makes his living guiding other anglers. A few years ago, after 20-plus years of hustling freight on loading docks in St. Paul, Minnesota, he quit and did what he always wanted to do—fish.

The Griz fishes all year. He guides on the Mississippi and St. Croix rivers in early spring, then spends the summer and fall showing fishermen the ropes on lakes in northern Minnesota and in Canada. His only break occurs during those few weeks between ice-up and the time when it is thick enough to support his weight. Then he is back at it, guiding ice fishermen with the same unbridled enthusiasm for catching fish that he maintains all summer.

Although The Griz has built a reputation as one of the best walleye fishermen in the country, he fishes and guides for any species. Northern pike are a favorite, even though his names for the pike, like "snake" or "scissor-bill," are less than flattering. The Griz likes pike because they grow big, are aggressive and provide a lot of action when other species might be reluctant to bite (like in midsummer, for instance). For a guide who makes his living putting fish in the boat, northern pike can be real trip savers.

Most anglers will tell you that midsummer is the most difficult period of all for taking many pike or big pike. You won't hear that from The Griz. He says that pike are almost always willing to hit; it is just a matter of putting something in their face which turns them on. And don't ever try to tell The Griz that you can't catch big pike in the midsummer heat. The man has caught more 10- to 20-pound pike in midsummer than most anglers will see in a lifetime.

How does he do it? What are his secrets? Well don't go looking for some hot new lure or previously unheard-of technique. The Griz is the best at what he does, in part, because he doesn't get wrapped up in gadgetry, gimmicks and fads. Instead, he sticks

Proper Action For Trolling Weedlines

Weedbeds are a good place to look for mid-summer pike. Gryzinski trolls the weedbeds in a weaving motion, rather than following the edge of the weeds. He says pike can be anywhere in the weeds.

to what worked for his parents who taught him how to fish. He relies upon time-proven techniques, solid but basic equipment and, perhaps most importantly, an uncanny knack for knowing where the fish are. It's the kind of sixth sense that only comes after many hours on the water.

Look For The Weeds

Northern pike hunt their prey from ambush. That means that they are most successful when they have some type of cover in which to hide. Weeds are a natural. While northerns will use any type of weed cover in lakes lacking cabbage, the best pike lakes nearly always have cabbage beds. To find them, The Griz relies on electronics, mainly his flasher. By turning the gain up until he gets a double echo, he can cruise the lake watching for that series of narrow blips indicating weeds below.

Once he has found the weeds, The Griz runs the weedbed or weedline until he knows exactly its configuration. Many of us have difficulty visualizing how something looks underwater, but The Griz is able to memorize not only the weedbed's precise location, but all the little nooks, pockets, inside and outside turns and places where the weeds are a little thicker than normal. When fishing a new lake, The Griz may locate six weedbeds and weedlines before even beginning to fish.

While all weeds hold some fish, on a good northern pike lake, the prime locations for big fish will be weeds adjacent to deep water. For instance, a large, 8-foot-deep flat may have scattered cabbage patches, but the most productive weeds will be found where the flat drops off into 15 feet of water. The bigger pike, it seems, take up the best positions in any weedbed, leaving smaller fish to make do with what's left.

Mid-Lake Humps

Most weedbeds relate to shoreline structure, usually points or flats. Weedlines are found at about the same depth throughout the lake, because sunlight must be able to reach the plants to ensure growth. For most anglers the search for pike-holding weeds begins and ends with locating the weedlines and obvious weedbeds. But not for The Griz. He is constantly studying maps and running over a lake in search of mid-lake humps.

"Find a mid-lake hump that has weeds around its fringe, kind of like the ring of hair around a bald man's head, and you just know there are going to be some pike there," he explains. "And since nobody ever takes the time to find these places, these humps usually hold a really good fish or two.

"Lots of times those big bruisers that spend a good share of the summer out in open water where they are virtually uncatchable will relate to a small, mid-lake hump," he continues. "They might not be there all the time, but they visit it often. I do the same thing, always checking back, making these humps part of my 'milk run.' Sooner or later that fish and I are going to be there at the same time, and then I've got him."

Jig-Fishing The Weeds

"Too many people never try fishing jigs in the weeds because they are afraid that they are going to be hung up on the weeds all the time," says The Griz. "Well sure, you catch a weed once in awhile, but most of the time you can just pop the jig free and get right on with catching fish. Guys who aren't fishing jigs in the weeds are really missing the boat when it comes to catching a bunch of pike."

　　　　Complete Angler's Library

Casting A Jig Into A Weedbed

The Griz often will pause to thoroughly work the pockets in a bunch of weeds. He casts the jig into the weedbed, retrieving it steadily until it reaches a pocket. Then he lets it free-fall into the pocket, as indicated in lower drawing.

The Griz uses both ¼-ounce and ⅜-ounce jigs for fishing the weeds. Surprisingly, the jigs are not the big ones with 1/0 hooks that are often sold for northern pike but the ones The Griz uses for fishing walleyes—Northland Fireball jigs with stinger hooks and a homemade jig. Most of the time The Griz doesn't bother to buy expensive sucker minnows for tipping his jigs, either. Instead, he relies on his old standby, the fathead minnow. He runs the hook point in the minnow's mouth and up through the top of the head right between the eyes. Fatheads have a very tough skull, so this hooking arrangement keeps the minnow on the hook even when it's being pulled through the weeds.

Getting the jig through the weeds requires ripping the jig forward anytime you feel it hang up on a weed. When you really pull back on the rod to tear the jig free, you accomplish three things.

One, you free the jig. Two, any weed strands clinging to the jig usually will be dislodged, so you don't have to reel in and clean the jig. And three, that sudden surge will often trigger a strike, and it's the kind of a strike which you probably will feel right down to your toenails.

Cast Or Troll

You can take northern pike on a jig by either casting or trolling. Which method The Griz relies upon depends upon the configuration of the weedline or weedbed.

"If I've got a fairly straight stretch of weedline," he says, "one without a lot of points and pockets, I drop a marker at each end of the stretch I want to fish and then troll over it a couple of times. When I troll, I weave in and out the whole time so that I am constantly putting the jig on the weedline's edge as well as up in the weedline. Although you read a lot of stuff about fish always relating to the weedline's edge, that is just not the case. Many times those scissor-bills will be tucked back in the weeds, especially during a cold front. If you just fish the weedline's outside edge like everybody else, you're never going to touch those fish.

"But now if the weedline is a real irregular one, with lots of points and bends," he continues, "I prefer to cast. And weedbeds, because they don't run in line like a weedline, are best worked by casting. Most of the time I'll catch more fish by casting than I will by trolling. I think it is because I can put a little extra action on that jig, kind of make it do what I want. Like pockets for instance.

"You take a good thick bed of cabbage weeds—maybe the size of a small house—and it is going to have a couple of pockets, or open areas in it. Well if you troll over the weedbed, your jig just keeps right on moving over the top of these pockets. That old snake might come zipping up to nail it, but he might not, either. Casting, I can let that jig free-fall down into those pockets. Pike just can't seem to resist a jig fluttering down through one of those openings," he says.

The Griz prefers spinning gear when he is jig-fishing for northern pike. Spinning gear makes it easier for casting the light jigs that he uses. It's usually the same outfit that he uses for walleyes. "I just add a foot of Melt-Twist leader material to the end of my line," he says, "tying my line through the loop and the jig on the other. Nothing fancy ... You don't need it."

Spoons, Cranks And Spinnerbaits

But The Griz is not solely a one-method fisherman. If the fish aren't buying his jigs on any given day, he may cast spoons, retrieving them quickly so they just slide on top of the weeds. Little Cleo's are a favorite, so are Dardevles, especially the hammered copper model with the orange stripe down the middle.

Spinnerbaits get the nod when he's fishing in junk weeds. He likes to retrieve them just fast enough to keep them above the weedtops; then he lets them free-fall into pockets. If the fish are really "off," he tips the spinnerbait with a small sucker minnow. White skirt/silver blade and black skirt/orange blade are his favorite colors.

Crankbaits, especially Rat-L-Traps, are his choice when he wants to troll a weedbed or weedline quickly to see if there are any active fish.

"Other fishermen have seen me trolling for northerns and have later come up to me at the dock to ask where the water-skier was," The Griz says. "Then they laugh because they think I troll way too fast. But a northern pike is incredibly fast, you can't troll too fast for those buggers. When I'm dragging cranks I want to cover a lot of water in a hurry."

When fishing spoons, cranks and spinnerbaits, The Griz uses a baitcasting rod and reel, 12-pound-test line and a steel leader.

Jerkbaits For Big Pike

"Jerkbaits start to produce big pike in the middle of the summer and then just keep right on getting better into the fall," says The Griz. "If you want a really big pike and don't really care about catching a bunch of smaller fish, then jerks are the way to go. There is something about that hunk of wood that really gets big pike going.

"Fishing jerkbaits takes a little practice, but once you get the rhythm down, it becomes automatic. Jerkbaits don't have any action on their own, so you have to make them dance the way you want them to. I like to get high in the boat by standing on the casting platform or up on a bench seat. On the retrieve, I keep my rod pointed at the water and pop the rodtip downward; at the same time reeling up the slack line. This makes the jerkbait jump ahead a couple of feet. By reeling quickly at the same time, I keep the slack out of the line. If there is slack in the line, it is almost im-

Gryzinski uses muskie tackle in working jerkbaits for big northerns. As shown here, The Griz' favorite lure has seen a lot of action and has the scars to prove it.

possible to get the hooks into a pike when it hits the jerkbait.

"Most of the strikes occur during the first couple jerks or right at the boat," he continues. "I always like to give the jerkbait a little extra action at the end of the retrieve, something to trigger that big pike that might have followed it all of the way in but needs a little extra incentive to come up and nail it.

"I'll tell you what, you get 20 pounds of pike smashing that wood at boatside with nothing but 5 feet of line between you and him, and you're talking pure excitement," he says.

The Griz uses muskie gear when tossing jerkbaits for big pike. He used a 5½-foot muskie rod, Garcia 6500 C casting reel and 36-pound-test dacron line with a steel leader between the line and the lure.

"There are times," says The Griz, "when pike won't have anything to do with hardware, times when nothing but the real thing will do the trick. That is when I like to drift a sucker minnow over a weedbed. My favorite method is to start on the upwind end of a weedbed and just let the breeze drift the boat across it. I drop a nice big sucker over the side and let it drift right along with the drift of the boat.

Complete Angler's Library

"The key to this kind of fishing is to adjust the float so that the sucker swims along over the weedtops and doesn't get down and bury itself. I like to hook it through the snout with a sharp 1/0 hook. A sucker hooked this way will live a long time. On a really big sucker, one that's a foot long, I will add about a ¼-ounce weight to the line to help keep the sucker down where it belongs. Smaller suckers need less weight.

"I don't like those big, round, plastic bobbers most people use. Cylindrical-shaped slip bobbers are much more effective. You can adjust the slip-bobber to the depth you are fishing," The Griz says. "It allows you to reel in without having to remove the bobber, and the slim shape means that the northern feels less resistance when he takes the sucker."

Striped And
White Bass

22

Tactics For Giant River Rogues

by Chris Altman

L ooking for hot striper action? Go up a river this summer. One look at a striped bass should tell you that it is a fish engineered from stem to stern to spend its life in moving water. Its long, torpedo-shaped body is designed to slice through the flow, while the striper's heavy musculature and broad tail provide the power to overcome the strongest currents.

In fact, saltwater striped bass spend their lives coping with the oceans' tides. Even their spawning ritual, which carries these fish miles and miles into our freshwater, inland rivers, is dependent upon a strong current to successfully hatch the eggs.

Even though these fish are perfectly at home in the currents, most American anglers overlook rivers and streams when hunting trophy stripers, preferring instead to float their boats on a placid reservoir. And, for the most part, those venturing into the rivers will limit their forays to the ever-popular tailrace areas below hydroelectric power-generation dams. But there is an entire striped-bass population which is virtually ignored by striper fishermen. They are river-run stripers, and they represent the last, secretive frontier of striped-bass angling.

A Game Of Hide And Seek

Anglers fishing tailrace areas, below some of our larger dams, might be surprised to learn that the dissolved-oxygen levels there are not high enough to support trophy-class stripers.

Arthur Kelso Jr., a striper guide and seventh-grade science

Arthur Kelso displays one of his river striper catches. He's able to find good-sized stripers where other anglers wouldn't think of looking.

Tactics For Giant River Rogues   257

teacher from Loudon, Tennessee, began fishing for river rocks in 1975. Watts Bar Lake had been stocked with the saltwater transplants, and the tailrace below Fort Loudon dam in the headwaters of Watts Bar was (and still is) a popular hangout for striper fans. "I fished for stripers there for several years but couldn't catch any over 25 pounds," Kelso says. "Most of the fish I caught were 10 or 12 pounds. I knew there were bigger fish there, so I began doing a little detective work."

A switch from the small, 3-inch, "log perch" minnows that most anglers used as bait to larger, 6- and 8-inch gizzard shad instantly doubled the average size of Kelso's catch. Still, the giants failed to attack Kelso's offerings.

"I asked a few fisheries biologists about it," Kelso said, "and one man told me that there was simply not enough dissolved oxygen in the tailwater areas to support bigger fish." (The water in most tailraces is pulled from the lake's bottom and has a very low dissolved-oxygen content, especially in summer. What is more, big fish require a higher level of dissolved oxygen in the water than do smaller fish.)

"He suggested that I go downstream about two or three miles and start looking for fish there," Kelso said. This was because surface water picks up oxygen from the air, and as the water rolls downstream, the boiling action imparted by the current mixes the water from top to bottom, thereby insuring a generous supply of dissolved oxygen.

Dave Bishop, an assistant regional manager for the Tennessee Wildlife Resources Agency and a recognized striped-bass expert, says, "Occasionally, some dams may have an oxygen problem that limits striper activity in the tailrace area. In most instances, however, I think that the reason larger fish are not caught has to do with the fish's nature rather than any kind of oxygen problem. It might be that larger fish don't like to fight the enormously strong tailrace current, although I have no concrete data to back that up. Too, as stripers increase in size, they prefer cooler water, so this might be a factor in some areas. Truly large striped bass are difficult to catch wherever they are found, and I think that component is involved in many areas frequented by anglers."

Whatever the case may be, Kelso knew that he was not finding the truly monstrous stripers that he was searching for, so he decided to venture downstream to uncharted waters. "I had no idea where to look," he said, "but I knew that stripers use the deeper river channel as a sort of highway to move from place to place. With that in mind, I started looking and drifting shad. To make a long story short, I started with 12 big shad. I hooked 12 fish in 12 drifts around this one island, and nine of them broke my line. I knew I had found my honeyhole!"

Kelso continued to experiment, developing a very successful system for fishing rivers. How successful? His average fish weighs 20 to 25 pounds, and his largest river striper to date is a 47-pound giant! News of his tremendous success spread rapidly, and Kelso now operates a striper guiding service during the summer.

Shallow Versus Deep Water

Kelso believes most anglers fishing a river for the first time doom themselves from the start. "When people think of stripers," Kelso explains, "they think of deep water, which is only natural because most anglers fish for stripers in a reservoir, and stripers tend to hold relatively deep in an impoundment. But in a river, anglers should be focusing their attentions on shallow water. You can find plenty of stripers in deep river holes, but they won't be feeding.

"Stripers spend most of their time in deep water. But in a river, there's not much to eat down there," he continues. "When river stripers get hungry, they move into shallow water. Most of my fish are caught in water less than 10 feet deep, and I catch a lot of fish in water as shallow as 3 or 4 feet."

There is a lot of shallow water in a river; common sense will tell you that you cannot simply fish it all. Kelso believes that a successful angler must target shallow water structure that stripers use as ambush points and feeding areas.

"I concentrate on the shallow, subsurface structure that breaks the current's flow," Kelso says. Luckily, these feeding holes are easy to locate. As you move downstream, watch for any kind of a surface boil. This will tell you that something is below the surface, breaking the current's flow and creating surface turbulence. It might be a big rock pile, a stump or an old car; it makes no difference. The key is that the structure is located in relatively shallow water and that it breaks the current's force.

"When you see a boil, go back upstream, shut off your big motor and drift over the boil while watching your depthfinder," says

Tactics For Giant River Rogues   259

Locating Striper Hotspots In Rivers

This shows how stripers will congregate around and in underwater obstructions such as stumps or rocks—anything that breaks the current's flow. Stripers wait to ambush baitfish.

Kelso. "What you are looking for is a change in depth. The water might go from 15 feet to 7 then back to 15 feet once you pass over the top of the object. This is a feeding hole, and sooner or later a striper will be there to feed. If there is a rockfish there, I guarantee it will hit your bait because it is sitting there for the sole purpose of feeding. If it wasn't hungry, it would be in deep water."

Fast Food For Giant Stripers

Of the many feeding holes Kelso has discovered, bridges are one of his favorites. "Bridge piers (pilings or abutments) are one of the most productive areas in any river for several reasons," he says. "One is that the pilings break the current's force. Bridges will usually have a lot of debris around them, because excess building materials and trash are often tossed over the side. The debris and pilings give the fish something to orient around, plus it attracts baitfish which feed on the algae growing there. Bridge piers are relatively easy to fish because you can pinpoint exactly where the fish will be.

"I will usually start at the first pier which is in shallow water and closest to the river channel," Kelso says. "These pilings are usually set at an angle to the current flow, and one side of the pier will have more current than the other. Without fail, the fish will be on the pier's side with the strongest current. They might be on the pier's front, in the downstream eddy behind the pier, or in the swift water along one side of the pier. Their location makes no difference. Wherever they are along that side of the pier, you can be certain that they will be facing into that swift current.

"Once I have decided which side of the pier has the swiftest current," he continues, "I move upstream, cut the outboard and begin my drift." Kelso allows his boat to drift with the current, using his electric trolling motor sparingly in order to keep the boat on course.

"You want the boat to pass within a few feet of the pier," he says. "But never let the boat bump it or you'll spook every striper

Working Bridge Pilings For Stripers

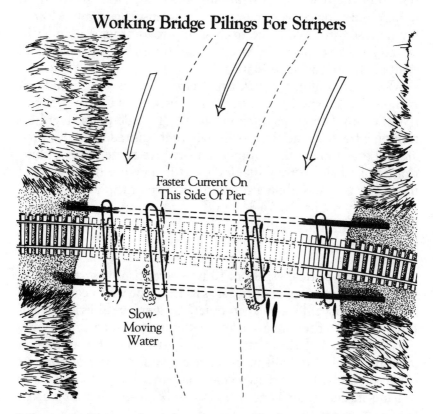

Faster Current On This Side Of Pier

Slow-Moving Water

Bridge piers, or pilings, are a favorite haunt for stripers. This shows how Kelso locates the stripers; they move along the side of the pier with the faster current.

in the area! Hold the rod in your hand and extend it out over the front of the boat as you drift. Bridges usually hold a lot of fish, so be sure to fish them thoroughly before you leave."

Another of Kelso's favorite striper hangouts is an island. "If the river you are fishing has a dam somewhere below it, and most do," he says, "chances are good that before the dam was impounded, the water level was considerably lower than it is now. The trees that were on the island's outside edges were more than likely cut so that they would not endanger boating traffic. This left a row of stumps underwater around that island.

"I believe these stumps are favorite feeding holes for stripers, especially for really big fish. For that reason, I work my way completely around an island, trying to hit every single stump I can locate. I have found that stripers tend to hold tighter to stumps than they do to any other structure," he continues, "so you need to make sure you get your bait right up against the stump. Most of my biggest fish have come from stump rows around islands. In fact, if I was going with the intent of catching a big striper, I would limit my fishing areas to islands."

To catch a monster rockfish, Kelso believes you should fish with big bait, something in the neighborhood of a 2- or 3-pound river herring (skipjacks, hickory shad). "I would put a river herring on a freeline and let it swim where it wanted while I drifted around the stumps. Big, trophy stripers love those big river herring, and I believe they hit one even if they are not hungry. I might not get more than a single run in two or three days of fishing, but when a fish hits a 3-pound river herring, you know it is a fish of trophy proportions!"

The Drift

The most critical aspect of Kelso's river fishing system is the drift. "Without a proper drift," says Kelso, "you won't catch fish."

Kelso's first rule is to keep quiet. Stripers are skittish by nature, and when they are just a few feet under your boat, nearly any noise will spook them. Never use an outboard motor around an area that might hold a fish; instead, use your electric motor, but use it sparingly. Don't slam a boat compartment lid, don't stomp or bang around in the boat, and don't talk any more than is absolutely necessary.

"Sometimes, just the boat floating over the fish will spook

Kelso is a believer in using fresh, live bait for stripers. This striper went after this yellowtail shad. If you want to catch big stripers, Kelso says, you have to use large bait.

them, so you want your bait to be the first thing which passes over the fish. For this reason, I always fish from the front of the boat and hold the rod in my hand. By holding a 7- or 8-foot rod, I can keep my bait 8 or 10 feet in front of the boat. By the time the boat passes over the restaurant, the fish has already hit my shad," Kelso says.

When a fish hits the bait, Kelso continues drifting with the current while fighting the tethered leviathan. Then when the fish is boated, he motors back upstream to a point above the structure, kills his big engine and drifts the spot again. Kelso often catches approximately two or three fish from around even a small piece of structure that way.

The Gear: Rods, Reels And Bait

One crucial component in Arthur Kelso's river system is healthy, live bait. "One of my favorite baits is a 5- or 6-inch yellowtail shad," he says, "but these are often very difficult to catch. Most of the time, I use 6- to 8-inch gizzard shad. But when I am after huge fish, I'll switch to 2- or 3-pound river herring (hickory shad)."

The most important thing about your live bait, Kelso believes, is keeping it healthy and vigorous. When using a long-handled dip net to catch shad, he does not try to catch a full net of shad because this may damage the bait. Instead, he will try to delicately pluck just two or three shad with each dip of the net. When using a cast net to gather bait, Kelso tosses the net to the outer fringe of the shad school in order to capture just a few fish with each throw.

"I choose only the strongest, healthiest-looking bait," Kelso says, "and I do not crowd them in my bait tank. As a general rule, I carry one shad for each gallon of water in my shad tank. When I use the really big shad, I reserve two gallons of water for each shad in my tank."

Because Kelso does most of his angling with just one rod (which he holds in his hand), he demands a lightweight rod that does not wear him out after 8 to 10 hours of fishing. His favorite rod is a 7½- to 8½-foot, graphite rod with a fairly limber tip. Although most striper fanatics put their faith in baitcasting reels, Kelso prefers a specific spinning reel made by Shimano. "Since Shimano introduced their Baitrunner reels, I use spinning gear almost exclusively," he says. "Shimano's Baitrunner reels allow a fish to take your bait and feel very little resistance. When you get ready to set the hook, simply flip a switch and the reel is kicked back into gear. In my opinion, the Shimano Baitrunner Model 4500 is the greatest thing to come down the pike for striper fishermen in years.

"I use 25- to 30-pound line when I am river-fishing because the water is fairly murky," he continues, "and I don't have to worry about it spooking the fish. Plus, I'm after big fish in thick, rough structure, so I need the strongest line I can get away with. I retie after every fish I catch, and I strip off 2 to 3 feet of line every time I retie. Also, I replace my line after every three or four fish I catch because the line tends to lose its stretch. Once that occurs, it becomes brittle and easy to break."

Kelso's terminal tackle rig is very simple. A 1-ounce egg sinker is slipped onto the line, and a strong, top quality 5/0 hook is tied to the terminal end of his monofilament. Next, a very soft lead split shot is crimped onto the line between the hook and the egg sinker so that the sinker rides about 18 inches above the hook. "When I use big river herring for bait," Kelso says, "I switch to a 10/0 shark hook, but I usually use these without a weight.

When To Go

Following the age-old indicator of springtime fishing activity, Kelso begins hunting hefty stripers in his favorite rivers when the dogwoods start to bloom. "As the lake downstream from the river warms up," he says, "the fishing in the river gets better and better because it stays quite a bit cooler than the main lake; stripers prefer a cool environment. The river also will have a much higher level of dissolved oxygen than will the main lake. This is because it is cooler, shallower and has a more distinct current."

Stripers are constantly on the move looking not only for baitfish, but for a comfortable environment as well. Thus, in summer months, you've got the larger population of main-lake stripers running up into the river where conditions are more favorable for them. This puts a tremendous number of fish in a smaller, relatively confined area, and that—as Arthur "Bear" Kelso has discovered—makes for some great fishing!

"My experience has shown that the most productive months for taking river stripers are July, August and September," Kelso says. "After that, the fishing gradually tapers off until the lake level has dropped. This will pull most of the fish in the river back down to the lake. You can still catch 10- to 15-pound fish below the dam throughout the winter, but when the big fish have left the river, I start deer hunting!"

23

White Bass

by Tony Mandile

Nestled among myriad stars, the full moon looked like a giant spotlight surrounded by thousands of tiny flashlights, all aimed at Arizona. Although the bright reflection off the water seemingly hinted dawn would arrive soon, I knew better. My watch told me it was only 4 a.m. The sun would not peek above the eastern mountains for at least two more hours.

The light from the graph on the console cast an eerie, greenish glow on Floyd Preas' face as he stared at the moving stylus. Taking a hand from the steering wheel to stifle a yawn, Preas spoke for the first time in 15 minutes. "Not much happening, huh?"

For several seconds, I wondered whether Preas was alluding to the obvious absence of other boats on Lake Pleasant, and I thought about answering with, "Maybe the really smart people stayed in bed this morning." When I leaned over and saw the fishfinder tracing a few, small inverted "V's," however, I realized Preas most likely was referring to the small number of fish showing up on the screen.

Preas once lived west of Phoenix and spent countless days chasing white bass at Pleasant, less than 30 miles from his front door. It's the only one of the state's inland fisheries harboring the whites. It was a rare day when he returned home without an ice chest filled with fish. He quickly garnered a reputation among his peers as the most knowledgeable and successful of Arizona's white bass anglers.

When you find white bass feeding, be prepared for some fast and furious action because it will be over almost as quickly as it starts. However, it's not hard to fill a stringer or ice chest.

White Bass

Although Preas later moved to the east side of the valley, more than 60 miles from Pleasant, and changed his focus to Apache Lake's smallmouth bass, he never forgot how to catch the whites.

Calling him a while back to learn about the top tactics for catching whites, I was invited to join him on a fishing excursion to witness his techniques first-hand. When he suggested I meet him at the launch ramp at 3 in the morning, though, I had second thoughts. "The fish have been chasing shad between 4 and 7 a.m.," he said. "If you want some real action, we had better be there before dawn." It was about 4 o'clock when the native Texan turned off the engine, pushed the brim of his trademark Stetson up a bit and leaned against the seat. "Let's sit a while and listen. Two days ago we ran into a huge school here and caught 37 before they moved out."

I simply nodded and listened to the slight splashing of the water against the boat—the only noise disrupting the early morning solitude. A sudden shiver caused me to think about pouring another cup of coffee to help remove the chill when I heard the noise and discovered Preas' judgment was prophetic. The raucous splashing was only 100 yards away.

"It's about time. I was beginning to wonder if I lost my touch." Firing up the big motor, Preas guided the boat slowly toward the chaos, shut off the motor again and hurried to the bow to lower the trolling motor.

The school of feeding bass had churned an acre-sized area of water into a turbulent froth. Hundreds of threadfin shad, their silvery sides reflecting the moonlight, bounced atop the water as they attempted to escape the hungry whites.

Preas lifted his foot from the trolling motor pedal and let the boat drift toward the melee. Like a gunfighter awaiting the moment his .45 would clear leather, he stood with rod cocked and ready in the boat's bow. As soon as the boat moved within casting range, he flipped the doll fly to the edge of the ravaging school. The tug of a strike immediately followed the soft "plop" of the lure hitting the surface.

Typical of white bass, the fish dove toward the bottom and swam from side to side. Using its deep body for leverage, it arched the light spinning rod into an upside down "U."

Preas saw me watching. "Don't wait for me. Catch a fish."

So I did—on the first cast. For the next 30 minutes, neither he

Although Fred Preas spends most of his time chasing smallmouths, it's not hard to coax him into trying his skills on white bass. He has developed a reputation over the years for being able to find and take white bass.

nor I stopped fighting fish. Frequently, we hooked fish at the same time. Then, just as suddenly as the huge marauding school had appeared, it vanished into the depths—a common scenario for white bass when their hunger is sated.

At the turn of the 20th century, white bass in North America primarily ranged from New Brunswick and Minnesota, southward through the Great Lakes region, St. Lawrence River and the Mississippi and Ohio Valleys. In the 1940s, however, the Bureau of Reclamation started building dams around the country resulting in big, sprawling reservoirs with perfect habitat for the whites.

Fisheries biologists soon realized how well the large impoundments suited the fish. They also learned the prolific white (called "silver" or "sandy" in some areas) could fill a niche in lakes where fish species were difficult to catch. In contrast, catching the white

White Bass

bass, because of its schooling tendencies, is relatively easy. In fact, it's almost a sure thing where populations are high.

The white bass can be somewhat of a savior, too. Preas cites a trip he made to Pleasant many years ago. Back then, he owned a small aluminum boat. When he and his fishing partner launched the boat, the outboard refused to start.

He still laughs when he tells the story: "We took turns cranking on that cantankerous thing for 15 minutes. But nothing we did or any amount of swearing helped. So we decided to give it up and head home. Then, just as we were ready to load the boat, I heard the commotion a couple hundred yards from the launch ramp. A school of whites was on a shad-chasing orgy.

"We ran to the truck, got our rods and tackle boxes and jumped in the boat. While my partner rowed, I rigged the rods and tied on white maribou jigs. We caught 24 bass before the fish finished their feeding binge. I looked at my watch after we loaded the boat. It wasn't even 7 o'clock yet."

Expanding Fisheries

Although nearly every state of the lower 48 now has at least one lake harboring white bass, the South and Southwest, from Georgia west to California, unquestionably lead the way in top fisheries.

Oklahoma's Lake Texoma, created by Denison Dam in 1944, was one of the first places where the white bass gained fans. After the lake filled, native fish in the Mississippi River drainage rapidly moved in. Texoma's subsequent angling bonanza prompted more plants of silvers into almost every lake in the state. By the mid-1950s, Oklahoma's anglers were hauling home more than 2 million pounds annually. In comparison, commercial fishermen took a measly .3 million pounds from Lake Erie, even though it is 25 times larger than the total area of all the lakes in Oklahoma.

The white bass in Arizona were somewhat of a newcomer, too, compared to other fish species. According to Preas, the Arizona Game and Fish Department (AGFD), seeking some diversity for the state's fisheries, first examined the feasibility for stocking the bass in the early 1960s. Once the department concluded it had an ideal candidate to fill some voids, it had to find somewhere to put the whites. The biologists chose Lake Pleasant because they thought it filled all the requirements.

It was large and deep enough and contained plenty of open water. The Agua Fria River and lots of rock rubble and gravel in shallow water offered adequate spawning areas. More importantly, though, Pleasant contained a plentiful food supply. In many of the fisheries where the silvers do well, their main menu item is either the gizzard or threadfin shad. The latter already was well established in the 3,500-acre reservoir.

At first the experimental stocking appeared to be a dismal failure. The whites seemingly disappeared for several years, causing the fisheries people to do some head-scratching. The concern was unfounded, however.

The bass obviously had hidden in the depths somewhere until they suddenly began grabbing lures. A few curious fishermen, unfamiliar with the species, called the game and fish offices and asked about their unusual catches. Some of these anglers, aware of the recent introductions of landlocked striped bass into the Colorado River lakes, assumed those stripers had somehow established themselves in Lake Pleasant.

AGFD told callers that Lake Pleasant never received any striped bass plants, so the mysterious fish had to be Pleasant's newest residents, the formerly elusive whites.

Preas said confusing the two species is fairly easy because a mature white bass (*Morone chrysops*) and a small striped bass (*Morone saxatilis*) look very much alike. Along with yellow bass and white perch, they belong to the temperate bass family—*Percichthyidae*. Even biologists once thought erroneously that the white bass was a landlocked, freshwater version of the common saltwater striped bass. Subsequent studies proved otherwise.

Identification became even more difficult in some fisheries with the introduction of crosses between the white and striped bass. These hybrids, often referred to as "wipers," appeared in 1965 as a result of experiments by biologists Dave Bishop of Tennessee and Bob Stevens of South Carolina. The first "wiper" release occurred at Tennessee's Cherokee Lake.

Experts say counting the rays in the soft part of the back dorsal fin is a sure way to distinguish a white from a striper at any age. The striper has 12 rays, while the white bass has 13. In mature fish, the differences are readily apparent. A striper possesses a relatively slim body, while the white bass appears deep-bodied through the middle, more like a crappie. Also, the striped bass grows to a larger size, occasionally exceeding 5 feet in length and more than 50 pounds in weight. The spunky white bass, in contrast, rarely tops 5 pounds, generally averaging between ½ and 2 pounds.

The International Game Fish Association (IGFA) currently lists a 6-pound, 13-ounce white bass from Lake Orange, Virginia, as the all-tackle world record, and only three, including the all-tackle record, top 5 pounds. So it's easy to understand why a 4-pounder rates trophy status. Arizona's largest and former IGFA world record, a 5-pound, 5-ounce fish caught at Imperial Reservoir on the Colorado River by a California angler, was a by-product of a transplant from Lake Pleasant, also the producer of the state's 4-pound, 11.5-ounce inland record.

One reason why white bass usually don't weigh more than 4 pounds is the species' short lifespan. Some occasionally live eight years, but most never celebrate a fourth birthday. They are cyclic but prolific spawners. Although the whites spawn annually, a good spawn might take place only every second or third year. However, one female can lay a million or more eggs. Left unchecked, they can rapidly overpopulate a lake and consume the available food supply. The average size drops dramatically when this happens. Most states, including Arizona, have no limit on them to prevent such upsurges. Fish in lakes with excellent baitfish populations, such as Pleasant, normally grow larger.

Methods For Finding Whites

Before the advent of improved fishfinders, Preas used three methods to locate bass schools. Although all are basically hit-or-miss, they rarely have failed to produce.

Preas calls his favorite technique jump-fishing—the way we accidentally found the fish on that chilly March morning while we were using a graph recorder in our search for them. He simply goes to a likely feeding area and either patiently waits in one place or slowly cruises, watching for telltale surface activity. Although whites might feed on top at anytime, the best bets for finding them are either early or late in the day. Binoculars make it easier to spot them in low-light conditions, and another tip-off, of course, is the noise. The sound of a feeding fling often carries up to a half-mile across the water on quiet, windless days.

Preas watches the sky, too. "It's a good idea to look for feeding

You can increase the fun and excitement by taking white bass on a fly-rod outfit. All you have to do is flip a doll fly to the edge of a ravaging school of bass and the fun begins.

birds," he says. "Gulls hang around many of the inland lakes and watch for the chance to scavenge. If the bass are banging a school of shad, there's plenty of dying baitfish on the water that the fish miss. So the birds grab them."

Trolling is another way to locate the schools. Preas thinks it's the ideal method during the summer months, especially in states like Arizona where the daytime temperatures almost always top 100 degrees. The heat typically drives the fish deeper, and they only feed on top during the cooler hours.

"Trolling to find fish depends upon finding the right combination of boat speed and lure," Preas says. "To be successful, you have to experiment. Try shallow and deep-running lures, and vary the boat speed accordingly. The bass will be suspended at specific depths where the water temperature suits them. Once you find

White Bass 273

them, though, the action can be exciting."

The whites' schooling tendency creates the excitement. If you catch one while trolling, others will be close. So taking a lure back through the same spot should attract additional strikes.

When a fish hits a trolled lure, Preas immediately shifts the motor into reverse and backs to the strike area to stay near the school. After you have the first bass in the boat, rather than trolling again, try casting jigs or lures to the surrounding area.

Preas often tosses out a marker buoy after he has backtrolled close to the spot where the hookup took place. Some anglers use a "chase" fish in states where it is legal. A fairly large float or small, barely inflated balloon with 20 feet of 6- or 8-pound-test monofilament attached to it is used with the line tied to the first fish caught. The fish is released as close to the hookup spot as possible, and usually rejoins the school. Then you can follow the bobbing float and catch more fish. Once the action ceases, retrieve the float and handline the first fish in.

When choosing lures, keep in mind that white bass can be very selective at times, particularly when they are not actively feeding. Over the years many lures have worked well for Preas, but they all had one thing in common: They imitated a threadfin shad—the white's meat and potatoes. For trolling, he recommends plugs such as Bomber's Ratl "RRR" "A," Smithwick's Water Gater, Whopper Stopper's Bayou Bogie, Cordell's Spot and Storm's Thinfin Shad. Small to medium-sized Rapalas also are effective.

The best one to use on any given day depends mostly on the depth at which the fish are located. Lure choice is not critical when the bass are on top, slashing up threadfin shad. Because most fish in a feeding school will be near the surface, lures should run fairly shallow. Yellow or white curly-tailed grubs on light jigheads or large doll flies are good choices. Shallow-running crankbaits or large Mepps or Panther Martin spinners will produce, as well. And for the ultimate excitement, try a topwater lure, such as Heddon's Zara Spook or Rebel's Pop R.

Preas suggests casting ahead of the surface action in the direction the baitfish are moving. "I avoid throwing into the middle of the school because it can spook the fish and send them down deep," he says. "And throwing a lure behind the feeding bass usually picks up only stragglers."

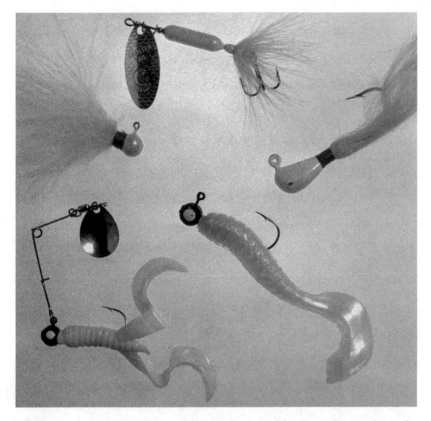

When you get into a feeding school, lure choice isn't a critical decision. Yellow or white curly-tailed grubs on light jigheads or large doll flies are all excellent choices.

A different technique is required in the cooler winter months, Preas says. And his graph-type fish locator is his main tool. "The hardest thing is finding the fish," he says. "Being familiar with a lake sure helps, though. Whites often hang around underwater structure, where the shad will be. So that's where I start looking for them. I just turn on the graph and slowly cruise the likely haunts. Once I find them, I decide on how to fish them and what lures I will use."

In most instances, his choices are jigging and a heavy spoon, especially when the fish are deeper than 15 feet or so. When he locates a bunch of fish on his graph, he anchors over the school and fishes right below the boat.

"I drop the spoon all the way to the bottom and reel it up a foot or two," he says. "If the fish are suspended way off the bottom,

White Bass 275

According to Preas, one of the keys to catching white bass is to not allow slack in the line. This means that anglers using fly rods will be doing a lot of hand striping to keep tension on the fish.

though, I drop it to that depth. Then I just slowly lift the spoon a few feet with my rod and let it fall again. The key is keeping the slack out of the line on the drop when many hits occur. No doubt, the bass see the spoon as an injured shad floating to the bottom. So they can't resist the free meal. Even though this is a good way to catch fish in the winter, it can work during other times, too, if the fish are deep."

When it comes to tackle, Preas always chooses light spinning rigs and 4-pound-test line. He claims he can feel the strikes better when jigging with this combination, and it allows him to cast farther which is important when working a feeding school. The more distance between the boat and the fish, the less chance there is of spooking the fish.

Sometimes no matter what a person does, nothing seems to

work. And Preas is no exception. "There have been a few times that I have gone to the lake after white bass and didn't find a one," he says. "It's all part of fishing. On the other hand, I would bet there are more whites caught accidentally than on purpose. It's all a matter of being in the right place at the right time.

"I remember a trip a few years ago. We went after largemouth, but it was one of those days when the fish had lockjaw. About 30 minutes before sundown, we were fishing plastic worms in Bill's Cove, one of my favorite places, and my partner finally got a bite. On the first jump, though, the fish spit the worm back at the boat. It was a good bass, too. I never saw Tom get upset at such things, but the fat bass clearing the surface and coming unhooked hit his hot button. He unleashed a tirade spiced with words not fit for the kids to hear.

"It was just before dark, and the cove was calm and quiet," he continues. "About the only sounds were the worms hitting the water as we made a few last casts before heading to the ramp. Then the whites showed up, and the water came alive.

"We rushed to take the worms off and tie on jigs. It was really funny, too. We dumped a tackle box on the floor of the boat and a pair of sunglasses went to the lake's bottom. When it was all over, we had more than 24 whites in the boat.

"To me, corralling a mess of whites in a cove like that and nailing one on every cast ranks right up there with the most thrilling experiences in freshwater fishing, even when it is an accident. It's really fun when every fish weighs close to 3 pounds," he says.

Index